DRIVE

SHIFT INTO RICH

Navigate the 9 Roadblocks to Small Business Success

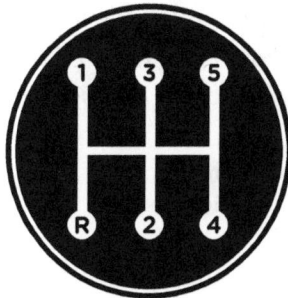

Diana Lidstone

Foreword by Peggy McColl, New York Times Best-Selling Author

I love how Diana brings clarity to building a fast track strategic profit plan so that you can accelerate your business to the next level. You'll feel the power in the drivers seat and know exactly what action to take when roadblocks appear. Apply her GPS system and you're on your way to riches.

Deborah MacDonald, Lifestyle Entrepreneur, Investor & Author
www.deborahmacdonald.com

This book is a must read for any entrepreneur or small business owner. Diana's real life experiences and honest revelations about her own business journey will inspire you to implement her teachings immediately so you too can have a wildly successful life.

Jayne Blumenthal
7-Figure Mindset Mentor, www.jayneblumenthal.com

Over my career as business consultant and coach, the one thing new entrepreneurs hated to hear is that less than one in five start-ups will still be around after five years. The reasons are complex and highly personal. With this book, Diana has condensed 30+ years of business experience and crafted an easy to follow road map of how to plan, implement and succeed in your business! This book is a "Foundational Biz Must Have!

Bob Carscadden CPA, CGA
Director of Finance and Administration
Ottawa Regional Cancer Foundation.

Shift into Rich is an incredible tool that every entrepreneur should have in their library. I wish I had her book 22 years ago because it addresses all the roadblocks that I've experienced in my business. The practical strategies and exercises that Diane so generously shares would have helped me move forward at a much quicker pace. If you are feeling stuck in your business or are starting out, Shift into Rich will give you seasoned expertise to guide you on your journey!

Catherine Bell,
PRIME Impressions
www.prime-impressions.com

Once I started reading Shift into Rich, I knew I had to read the whole book. As a seasoned business owner, it forced me to take a minute (many in fact) to reflect on my own business journey. I recognized the road blocks that I have personally struggled with and overcame...largely through trial and error. I realized that I had wasted a lot of time trying to figure things out on my own. In a nutshell — I loved the book! It's a great resource for any business owner to have in their library to refer to again and again.

Daniel Roy CFP, EPC, CIM, FCSI, CIWM, CRC
President, Praxis Wealth Management

This is a great easy-to-read book with key concepts for any entrepreneur! Diana outlines activities that people NEED to do if they are going to have any chance at being successful. Although these concepts are not sexy, they make up for it by being simple understand and to execute. Distilling these concepts into bite size, easy to understand chapters can only be done by someone who has been through the entrepreneurial journey and succeeded. Congratulations Diana!

Greg Weatherdon, Author and Small Business Expert
www.gregweatherdon.com

ISBN: 978-0-9958195-0-4
Emporium Marketing Consultants Inc.
40 Vanston Road
Mallorytown, Ontario, Canada K0E 1R0
www.dianalidstone.com

Published in Canada

Dedicated to those who believed I could

So that now I believe YOU CAN!

Acknowledgements

A common proverb notes that, "It takes a village to raise a child". Having come this far in the writing process, I can truly say that it also "takes a village" to write a book. However in retrospect, it isn't just about writing the book, it's about what brought me to the place where I knew I *could* write a book. Thousands of individuals, friends, family members, clients, prospects, naysayers, supporters contributed to my belief that I could write a book that would help others.

However, more than any others, I would have to say that it's the members of my family who have helped me the most. It's their unwavering belief, constant support and, yes, even financial backing, that I am truly grateful to have behind me. To my husband, Scott, my children, Lauri and Aaron, and those who have passed through this universe beside me: thank you. Words can't express how truly grateful I am.

I'd like to remind you, the reader, that there is someone in your world who truly believes in you; who believes you can do anything you want, who holds a bigger vision for you than you hold for yourself. Let yourself believe and be grateful.

Contents

Foreword

Diana Lidstone has created a remarkable gift for you all wrapped up in this book. This is a businesswoman, who created business after business, experiencing phenomenal success. And, as it is said: "if she can do it, you can do it".

You will be amazed with the incredible struggles that Diana went through as she was starting and growing her businesses. Some people think that people who start businesses have everything aligned ... all funds in order, plans in place, and strategies carefully crafted and ready to execute. In the "real world" that is quite often not the case.

You do not need to wait until everything is perfect or your plan is in place or having the funds ready to be put to work. If you have an idea, and you are ready to take action and believe in yourself and be willing to bet on yourself, you are good to go.

One of the greatest gifts we have all been given is the gift of choice. You can choose to have a successful business. You can choose to be rich. Now if any part of that statement is a challenge for you to believe, then I suspect you aren't enjoying the abundance the universe has to offer you. Please don't misunderstand me ... that is not a judgment but a simple observation. Most of the population is struggling financially. In fact, studies have shown that 97% of the people are earning 3% of the money. So, that leaves us to believe that 3% of the people are earning 97% of the money.

The truth is that even if we took all of the money in the world and spread it around evenly, it would still end up in the hands of those that have it now. Riches is attracted to people. Success is attracted to people. In order for anyone to experience success and/or riches, they must first believe it is theirs. As James Allen, the great philosopher said: "As a man thinketh in his heart, so is he."

Dive into this exceptional book and be ready to be inspired. Diana declares the reason why she wrote this book and who she wrote it for, but I believe this book is for anyone who has a desire for more and for anyone who has a desire to create success in their life.

I am grateful for Diana writing this book and you will be too. You will learn a lot about yourself by going through this book. And, if you have someone in your life that you deeply care about, please get them a copy of this book as well. This is not a book you will want to loan out to another as you'll want to keep it close by. This is a book you'll want to keep as your potential business guide. May you be blessed with an abundance of success in everything you do.

Peggy McColl,
New York Times Best-Selling Author
aka "The Best Seller Maker"
peggymccoll.com

Introduction

I think I know you pretty well. You're very smart, probably a life-long learner and perhaps a bit of a learning junkie. You're creative. You want something more from your business. And I'm betting that you're a woman (or one of the few brave men I've encountered). You created your business because you knew you could help others in a better way. And yet, you recognize deep down that something is stopping you from reaching the level of success that you want. You might even feel stuck, overwhelmed or just scared. You might feel as though you are on a hamster wheel because you just can't get enough accomplished in a day or you believe that you just don't have the business skills that you need in order to move forward.

I get it because I've walked in your shoes – whether they are sneakers, stilettos, or work boots; whether they are a size 5 or a size 10!

My Story

Thirty years ago, I started my first business when my son was still in diapers. I started it because I was tired of getting up at 5:00 a.m., dropping an infant off at daycare and travelling an hour in the dark to an office to work for someone else. I started it because I knew I could do better. I knew I could help others. So, over the years, I've started and built five profitable businesses.

My first business, in 1983, was a version of today's virtual assistant. Personal computers were just starting to hit the market and, as a trained executive secretary, I knew I could offer sales representatives, consultants, etc., a timely answer to their typing and secretarial needs. A business was born. It grew and prospered for two years.

Then my husband got transferred while I was pregnant with our daughter. Not to be deterred, I started my business again in a new city and I persevered. Finally, I found the key to success for Fall River Typing Service. This time it really grew. I hired staff, worked nights, took my reluctant daughter to daycare and prospered!

Four years later, my husband was transferred again! OMG - I didn't think I could start a business all over again. So when the children went off to school, I started working with horses as I had done while I was a student at university. I was well-paid. My kids thought it was odd to be paid for something I loved doing (little did they know they were learning an important quality of being a successful entrepreneur).

But again, I longed for more! I wasn't sure what "more" was, so I followed a retail path. A friend of mine had started a gift store. I borrowed her vision and started my "Vermont-style" country gift store. Within a couple of months, my husband and I had bought a building, attended some gift shows, found an employee and bought inventory (that part of the story could be a whole book on its own)! After a few years, I realized that my friend's vision of the store wasn't really my vision. I had to massage that dream into my own, and I had to do things my way. Emporium Hudson then morphed into a home decor store similar to the Pottery Barn. It really prospered! But eventually all good things come to an end. The day we left the building for the final time, I cried. I felt as though I were leaving a good friend. That building and the business had given me so much more than money. It had been my life for twelve years.

Oh and did I forget to tell you that during those 12 years, my daughter was ill and bedridden for seven years? My father died and my brother was found dead! Life certainly does know how to throw us challenges! But for each one of those challenges, I learned how to be stronger, braver and a better person. I learned that those were not challenges but, indeed, growth opportunities. I learned how to grow a profitable business.

I share my story with you so that you understand that I know about your challenges and your roadblocks! I know how hard it can be to raise a family and juggle a business, to have others who depend on you, to be surrounded by negativity. I know how hard it is to learn all the new skills that are required to grow a successful business. I know how scary it can be to leave the corporate world and strike out on your own. I know that to grow a profitable business takes time, often a lot of money, and personal growth.

My Why

But here's why I'm writing this book. Along the way, over these last 30 years, I've watched hundreds of women struggle to build profitable businesses. They started businesses with a dream, only to close their doors in debt. They started a business based on their passion, but didn't know how to turn it into profit. I've met business owner after business owner who couldn't turn a profit! It's not only puzzled me; it's also made me extremely sad!

It makes me sad because it isn't necessary. Today, women are starting businesses more than ever, and each one of them deserves to be successful. Each one of them deserves to *Shift into Rich*, to build a business that will support the life they desire. When I began my retail store in 1995, I knew nothing about retail. Nothing about inventory turns, hiring staff, purchasing, retail dating programs, profit margins, or budgeting. But I learned. Many of the things I learned were the result of mistakes that cost me either lots of money or lots of time.

Today the world is filled with information. A confusing amount of information. Tons of information is certainly available on how to build profitable business. There's a seemingly never-ending supply of books, videos, and online courses. Some of the information is free; some comes at low cost. There are even government agencies offering very low cost educational resources on business building! So why do four out of five businesses fail within five years? Why do women struggle to build profitable businesses when help is so readily available?

Not long ago it became my passion (and my mission) to help one million women grow profitable businesses. You see, along my journey, several people have held a bigger vision for me than I held for myself. They believed in me in a much bigger way than I believed in myself. So it's my turn: I believe in you. I'm going to hold a bigger belief in you than you hold for yourself. You can do this!

This Book is Different

When I decided to write a book, I wanted to write it for women, about business...but from a different perspective. There are hundreds, perhaps thousands, of business books available that deal with every imaginable business topic: client creation, online and offline marketing, how to use this social media or that social media... Yet, so far, I have not come across one business book that showed business owners the unseen roadblocks that might stand in their way, and give them advice to help avoid them.

This is a book about the roadblocks that no one told me about as I was building my businesses. It's a book about creating a road map for your business journey, one that will *anticipate* and *avoid* those roadblocks. It's a book to show you how to stop struggling so you can navigate your way to success with more ease (and perhaps a little fun along the way). There is a way to grow a profitable business without all the struggle.

Struggle Is Optional!
Diana Lidstone

The Entrepreneur's G.P.S.

You might be wondering why I call these challenges roadblocks? I've always been a rather visual person. I see big picture stuff. I envisage growing a business as being akin to taking a road trip. There's a starting point and a destination. It's a long journey but you are in the driver's seat. After all, it is your business. So throughout this book, you'll notice many analogies to travel: mapping out a trip, the roadblocks themselves, and the car in which you travel. After all, I am the Entrepreneur's G.P.S. I'm here to guide you so that you can reach your version of success.

What Can You Expect from this Book?

This is a business book but I promise not to fill it with technical terms that no one wants to hear. I promise to give you easy-to-follow exercises, tools and skills to navigate past the roadblocks. I promise that each chapter will have implementable action steps.

I'm passionate about action steps because I know that lack of information isn't the problem. It's putting that information into action that will help you make the changes you want in your business. It's action steps that will move you along your journey to success!

However, one book can't tell all. One little book can't possibly teach all or provide all the answers. One small book isn't the whole solution; it's only the tip of the iceberg. I think you'll agree once you've finished reading! I don't want to disappoint you, but growing a profitable business is a journey ... there's always more work to be done!

The Nine Roadblocks

This book will cover nine common roadblocks that creep up for every small business owner I've ever met. They seem to appear whether you're just dreaming about starting a business, whether your business is new, or whether you are ready to upscale and double your revenue. I'm going to write this to you, the woman who has a big heart and yet a bigger commitment to make a difference in the world; the woman who wants to make a bigger impact, bigger influence and a bigger income!

Quickly, here are the roadblocks you can expect to encounter as you travel along your business journey. I've broken the topics down into a couple of sections.

Your Road to Successville
1   Short-Sightedness
2   Wrong Activity, Wrong Time
3   Wandering Aimlessly

When you look at those topics, you might think they sound rather simple and easy to avoid. However, they aren't! I know, and so do my clients, and so do the many women I've spoken with over the years. You might surprise yourself.

Growing a profitable, successful business is the best personal development course you will ever take. Believe me. Along the road to your successes, you'll learn more about yourself than you ever anticipated. I call this mastering the inner business game. This involves becoming aware and learning about your inner voice (or as I call it, the Itty Bitty Shitty Committee). It's about playing from your strengths and inner gifts. It's about welcoming your inner wise woman. No one told me that any of these would be passengers in my car on my business journey!

There's also the outer business game and roadblocks that we don't anticipate. What I share here are the roadblocks that I see cropping up over and over again for small business owners. Often it's where you need new skills to move you ahead, such as learning about what key metrics are important to measure, discovering how to create clients and building a profit plan.

Grab a cup of tea (or a glass of wine), a pen and some paper. And let's get started!

Success comes from putting knowledge into action!

Diana Lidstone

Section 1
Your Road to Successville

ROADBLOCK #1: Short-Sightedness

You just won the $40 million lottery. After the shock and surprise wears off, and the celebrations finish, you and your partner decide to spend six months traveling around the world. How amazing is that? You start to dream about it. You decide to buy a large world map to put up on the wall. You start placing pins on the map to identify all of the places you want to visit. You start plotting out your destination. You realize that budget is not a factor so you decide to travel first class all the way – you'll enjoy the best hotels, the most luxurious spas, the finest dining. It's going to be all about luxury! You decide to throw caution to the wind.

You dream about this trip and you dream about it some more. And every time you dream about your trip, your vision for your six months of traveling gets clearer and clearer. Finally you decide that you've got it all figured out, right down to the details of your luggage and what you're going to wear. Now you're ready to go to the travel agent so that she can figure out *how* all of this will come together. She is going to do the planning and turn your dream into reality.

Okay – wake up!!! Snap back to reality! Remember—you are an entrepreneur; you own your own one-woman show. You're really busy – you spend your days putting out fires, making sales, handling customer issues and serving clients. Although your business is doing okay, you really want to increase sales and have an even bigger impact in the world. Perhaps you even want to double or triple your revenue. How? Who has time for thinking and planning about how it's all going to happen?

ROADBLOCK #1: Most business owners DO NOT take the time to develop a *Detailed Dream* for how they want their business to look in the future! Or what their business will look like when they've finished with it! Having a *Detailed Dream* will keep you focused on where Successville is located.

Here's what I know for sure …. If you are a one-woman show (or perhaps you have one or two assistants), I understand your challenges because I've spoken with and worked with business owners just like you. In fact, before I started my coaching business, I took time to specifically talk to several successful business owners and I asked them about their biggest business challenges. I also asked them where they saw their business three or five years down the line. Their answers astounded me. Nine out of 10 of these smart women told me that they had never given it much thought! They were busy working in their businesses but they had not defined what "success" meant for them

Have you defined your version of success? Where is Successville located for you? What does it look like? Where is it on the map? If you can't define "success," then how will you know when you've reached it? How will you know what activities to focus on so that you reach that level of success?

Without a *Detailed Dream*, or "vision," business owners tend to wander an aimless path. Overwhelm and frustration become their best friends. They end up on the hamster wheel, often burnt out or broke!

Let's go back and revisit the first paragraph of this chapter. The fantasy about winning the $40 million lottery relates to your business as well. I'd like you to notice three points of connection:

1. I used the word decide quite frequently in that lottery description. A *Detailed Dream* helps you make decisions because you have a clear idea of what you want to achieve.

2. The word *dream* is of great importance as well. I encourage you to take time to dream about where you want to take your business in the future. Don't focus on *how* it's going to happen — that part comes later. But make time to sit and think quietly, and to dream. That's called working *on* your business.

3. It's imperative that your dream business fits into the lifestyle that you want to create. Did you notice in the first paragraph that I said that there's no budget? You just won $40 million dollars and that's your new life, that's your new reality. How does your business fit into the reality that you want for yourself? As author Lewis Carroll once said, *"If you don't know where you're going, any road will get you there."*

We know anecdotally and from research that the power of visualization is very effective. Olympians use it to see themselves finishing the race or actually standing on the podium receiving a gold medal. We know that successful salespeople use visualizations to see themselves closing a million-dollar sales deal. History has shown us that people like Martin Luther King—who so famously said, "I have a dream"—know how the power of a dream can lead a nation. So why is it that we are reluctant to dream about what our business might be like in the future?

As women, we very often think we know what we want. Perhaps it's a successful career and a happy marriage. But then we get busy with life. We become busy helping others, and putting others first. We don't take the time to actually define what we mean by either success or happiness. Most of us never stop to think, period—to really discover what we want. We never stop to reward ourselves or to give our businesses the benefits of defining our success. As women, we often feel that we're hemmed in by what we think we should do. Let's, just for a short time, leave all those "should" behind us.

What Is a *Detailed Dream*?

So why is creating a vision for your business so important? Why is it that we should know what we're building? Creating a *Detailed Dream* — essentially a big picture vision — is like knowing the destination of your road trip. When you know where you are going, you have focus. Without focus, you wander and you are easily distracted. It's like being on the proverbial hamster wheel just going round and round and not getting anywhere—not making the sales, not having that bigger impact, and not having the influence that you want so that you can help more people.

A *Detailed Dream* gives a business direction and guidance. I see many entrepreneurs get so busy in their businesses that they continue to do the same things year in and year out. They are consumed by busy-ness and yet they don't seem to grow. A *Detailed Dream* gives them guidance so that they can carry out the kind of actions and strategies that help them grow towards their version of success!

Lack of vision is one of the biggest roadblocks that business owners encounter. It's one of those **Foundational Biz Must-Haves** (more on those later!) that business owners don't take time to develop. I can almost hear you saying "but I have a business plan!" A *Detailed Dream* isn't a business plan. It's an emotion-fuelled vision of where you want to take your business. It has no information on "how" you will do it. That comes later as well!

As a business owner, you are the leader of your company, the CEO. It doesn't matter if you have no employees or 20. How can you possibly lead without direction?

Can you give directions without having a destination?

Diana Lidstone

A vision comes from you, the company leader. It reflects your passion and it uses your excitement to fire up everyone else around you. It gets others excited at the prospect of learning from you, buying from you and working for you. As the leader, it's important for you to be able to plant one foot in the present and one foot in the future. You need to use your imagination to see into the future: to see your future sales, your future impact, your future influence. As a leader, it's up to you to become like former American President John F. Kennedy. He said he wanted to put a man on the moon and then managed to get his whole country behind his vision.

Do you want more from your business than you're currently getting? Do you want to double or triple sales? Do you want to have a bigger impact, and help more people? Then you need one essential discipline and that's Focus. Focus comes from having a *Detailed Dream* and then working to achieve it.

BIG thinking always precedes BIG achievement

Growing a prosperous business is a big achievement. So is climbing a mountain. A mountain climber's first decision is that, yes, they are going to climb a mountain. Next, they might decide which mountain they're going to climb. Will it be Mont Orford in Québec (853 m) or Mount Everest in Nepal (8,848 m)? This ONE decision affects everything else that follows!

So let's take this a little further. If you were the mountain climber and you decided to climb Mont Orford in Québec, preparations might include figuring out which trail you would take on your hike/walk, what day of the week you would pick for your climb, and perhaps you would make sure you check on the weather. You might decide that you're going to buy a new pair of hiking boots. On the day of the hike, you decide to pack a bottle of water and some snacks. Fairly simple. Not much else is required. You've made the decision and you worked backwards from your decision to climb Mont Orford.

But what if you had decided to climb Mount Everest? This is a much bigger endeavor requiring much more detailed planning. This climb is very weather-dependent. It would also require physical training in order to be in the best shape possible for the climb. You have to become part of an organized group—which group should you join? The budget, the clothing and the whole planning process would be very different for a Mount Everest climb than for a Mont Orford climb. However, the process would be the same: you would decide which mountain you're going to climb and then you would work backwards from that decision. It's just the details that would be very different.

I hope you can see the analogy between growing your business and climbing a mountain. You have to decide where you want to end up! You have to decide what you want to build. Okay, so I can already hear you saying, "Well, that's great, but how can I do all that? When am I going to find the time?" Do I dare suggest...make the decision to make the time! It will be a worthwhile investment and will save you time in the end.

How to Create a *Detailed Dream*

I lead each of my clients through a seven-step process to build their *Detailed Dream*. (Use the template for Detailed Dream found at www. dianalidstone.com/bookresources).

Briefly, here's how it works:

STEP 1. Book time away from your office with the specific intention of building your dream. Get away from all distractions. Go someplace where your creativity can soar. You might go by yourself, take your team, or attend one of my upcoming *Shift into Rich* Biz Getaways—just make sure that you leave the familiarity of your office and your home behind.

I remember when my husband and I had our retail store. At least twice a year we would disappear for a bit of a retreat and go to our favourite hotel where we would spend time dreaming about how our business would look in the upcoming years. It was a time to nurture our souls and to be more creative, to think outside the box. It did us a world of good and our business benefitted dramatically as a result.

STEP 2. Pick a time frame. What do you want your business to look like in six months, 12 months, and three years from now? I know that for many of you, it might be difficult to dream that far into the future and it may depend on the stage of your current business growth. If you are just starting out in business, perhaps you can really only dream three or six months into the future. However if your business is a little more settled (maybe you've done some market research and testing, and you're starting to make some money), then you certainly can dream at least 12 months into the future. If your business is a little more mature, say you've been in business for from three to five years, you can create a vision for what your business is going to be like three years into the future. Some business owners will even dream 10 years into the future. Pick a timeframe that is comfortable for you. A *Detailed Dream* can always be changed and updated! It's a dynamic document.

STEP 3. Be sure to include in your *Detailed Dream* something I call a "Leap"—something that will stretch you outside of the ordinary, outside of your comfort zone! Is it speaking on a stage in front of 100+ people? Is it writing a best-selling book? Is it franchising your business or taking it public? And yes, I know, you are going to say things to yourself like, "Who am I to do that?" or "Why do I think I'm capable of that?" (If that resonates with you, see Chapter 7.) That's just fear talking, and that's okay. Recognize the fear. Feel the fear. It's a hint that you're about to grow! You don't need to figure out "how" you are going to Leap now; just include it in your *Detailed Dream*. (By the way, writing this book was a "leap" of mine and I procrastinated for two years before I finally got into action!)

> *Don't wait for the fear to stop before you leap.*
> *Be willing to leap afraid*
>
> Lisa Nichols

STEP 4. Get started! Ask yourself some of these questions to start the process of dreaming about business in the future:

- What do you stand for? Why do you exist? What's your purpose?

- Why are your products/services important? (Ask and answer this question five times, going deeper each time.)

- If you had all the money in the world, would you still keep doing what you are doing? Why?

- What BIG goals do you want to accomplish? (Specific, clear, time sensitive, measurable)

- What are you best at doing?

- Describe what it would be like to achieve your BIG goals. How do you feel?

- How many clients will it take? If someone were writing an article for a major business magazine about your company in five-to-ten years, what would it say?

- What kind of people are in your life? How do you feel about them?

- What does your ideal day look like?

- Where are you? What will you be doing? Are you alone? Do you have a team?

- What does your business look like and feel like on this date in the future.

STEP 5. Share your *Detailed Dream* and encourage feedback. Share it with employees, with your significant other, or your mentor/coach. Getting feedback is important for two reasons. First, if you have a team, they need to understand what it is that you want to accomplish; they need to buy into your dream in order to be effective; they need to know that they are part of a bigger picture. Secondly, almost always, someone you share your dream with will tell you to DREAM BIGGER! They believe in you and they can see a bigger version of yourself than you can see. Trust them. Dream Bigger! (Oh, and yes, there will be others who say the opposite – your saboteurs. That's okay—you've got this!).

STEP 6. After the feedback, re-write your *Detailed Dream* in the present tense – as if it were happening right now. If you downloaded the *Detailed Dream* template, you'll notice that it's short! Keep it short so that you can read it every day, and so that it's easy for your team members to read frequently! By reading it daily, you'll start believing in it and you'll be more likely to focus your actions on achieving your dream, rather than becoming distracted. Visualize your dream as complete.

An example might be:

> *I have arrived! The year is 2020 and I have reached these exceptional milestones:*
>
> • *My annual sales are $800,000 with a profit margin of 65%.*
>
> • *My partner is thrilled to be working with me as the CFO and COO.*
>
> • *Four to six times a year, I speak on stages for large corporations and associations who pay me handsomely.*
>
> • *I'm thrilled to be hosting my own three-day live event in my home town, and people travel internationally to attend it.*
>
> • *Well-paying clients are eagerly attracted to work with me privately and through my retreats.*
>
> • *My online coaching program easily fills automatically, and provides an outstanding 30% of my income.*
>
> • *My best-selling books continue to fly off the shelves around the world helping small business owners reach success on their terms.*
>
> • *I continue to increase the quality time I spend with my children and grandchildren, friends and other relatives!*

STEP 7. Take consistent action! Dreams remain simply dreams unless you take action to bring them alive! So you're saying, "Well this was only supposed to be a dream. I don't know what action to take. I don't know how to make it reality." That's okay. Read on. I'll show you later (Chapter 3) how to take the dream and create a stress-free money making plan. But you need the *Detailed Dream* first!

Roadblock #1 - Shifting Actions

1. Block off time now in your agenda to create your *Detailed Dream*.

2. Download the *Detailed Dream* outline and start the process (www.dianalidstone.com/bookresources)!

3. Read your *Detailed Dream* daily.

4. Share your *Detailed Dream* with your team regularly.

5. Align your actions with your *Detailed Dream* daily.

Just a reminder ... this is your vision for your business. It's a vision for how you want your business to support your life. This vision comes from you ... from your core values, from your strengths, from your imagination, and from your uniqueness. So as you build this *Detailed Dream* for your business, remember to focus on who you are and what you do best. Don't judge yourself. Don't copy someone else's vision. There is no one right or wrong vision. There is no perfect *Detailed Dream*. Two people will never have the same version of "success."

Where is your "Successville" located?

ROADBLOCK #2:
Wrong Activity, Wrong Time

Your business journey starts in Nowville – that's the place on the map where you are currently located. You are in the driver's seat. If you've done the exercises in Chapter 1, you also know where Successville is located. Perhaps now you are wondering where to focus your attention, time and money. It's so confusing out there! There's a buffet of marketing and sales strategies to choose from, so many experts to listen to, and so many courses to take and investments to make. You feel like you don't know what to do next or what to try next! Congratulations: you've hit Roadblock #2!

ROAD BLOCK#2: Small business owners are spending far too much time doing exactly the wrong activities for their stage of business growth! Working on the right activities for your stage of business growth gives you time to work on the right activities for better results.

Over the years, I've noticed that the biggest problem for coaches, consultants, and service-based professionals is that most of them are spending far too much time doing exactly the wrong activities at the wrong time, and then wondering why their businesses aren't growing. I continually see small business owners struggling to create clients. They're having a tough time getting the word out about their business and they wonder if they are on the right track. Very often they are using strategies that just don't work for their level of business growth.

Let me share a couple of examples with you. About a year ago, I met a wonderful woman, Mary, who had written a best-selling book and yet she expressed frustration that she wasn't making any money! I was puzzled. After further conversation, Mary told me that she had spent tens of thousands of dollars writing and marketing her book. Not only that, she had spent more than a year writing it and promoting it. Still no significant revenue.

What was wrong with Mary's picture? Several things came to my attention. First, Mary didn't have any programs to sell after she had written the book. She had no email list she could use to sell programs or books. And she spent her hours attending networking events talking about her book. So you see: she had a book but nothing else. A better use of her time, money and energy would have been to develop programs, an email list and clients first, and then write the book. Unfortunately, she was busy with the wrong activity at the wrong time.

Here's another example. You've probably met several individuals like Lisa on social media. Lisa had a full-time job and I asked how I could support her in growing her business so that she could leave her job. Lisa's answer: "Oh, I'll just create an online course and sell it on the internet." The internet is a big place! Again, this was the wrong activity for Lisa's current stage of business growth. Don't get me wrong – there's nothing wrong with an online course, but you need a significant following/tribe/ community to make it successful. If you are just starting out, and decide to invest considerable time and money in an on-line course, you'll likely get very little return on your investment.

If so many business owners are doing the wrong things in the wrong order, how do you know where to focus your energy? The answer is simple: focus on the appropriate marketing and sales strategies for your level of business growth. The fact is that the strategies that you use as a "newbie" aren't the strategies you'll use as the CEO of a larger business.

*The strategies that you use as a newbie in business
are not the same strategies you will use as your business
grows!*

Diana Lidstone

Build Your House from the Bottom Up

Let me share the analogy of a house under construction. I'm sure that you realize that the contractor who lays the foundation, as well as the concrete guys, the roofers and the electricians, each have plans of action and approaches that are very different than those of the kitchen cabinet contractors. Right?

You also probably realize that the foundation needs to be correctly laid before the walls are constructed, the windows go in and the roof goes on. Right .... There's a sequence to how things go together.

It's the same for your business. The foundational elements need to be in place before growth can take place, and these require different strategies and methods.

Grow-Meter™

Introducing my proprietary business *Grow-Meter*™, which has helped me transform my coaching business from a few hundred dollars a month to several thousands of dollars a month. This concept has also helped hundreds of other business owners conquer their feelings of overwhelm. It has helped them focus their time, money and energy on appropriate actions that produces results, and allow them to take other inappropriate activities off their plate.

The *Grow-Meter*™ will help you to identify where you are in a typical business growth pattern. Once you determine your stage of business growth, you'll be able to focus on the right activities for your stage of business growth and to take off your plate those activities which aren't appropriate.

The advantage of all of this is that you'll be able to grow a profitable business strategically. You'll understand where to invest your time, your money, your energy and your focus. You'll be able to eliminate distractions so that you get more done and generate better results! When you are more focused on activities that bring you results, you'll feel happier, more confident. Frustration and overwhelm almost disappear.

G.P.S GROW-METER™

LEGACY

CEO

$_____

MANAGER

$_____

$_____

GLORIFIED EMPLOYEE

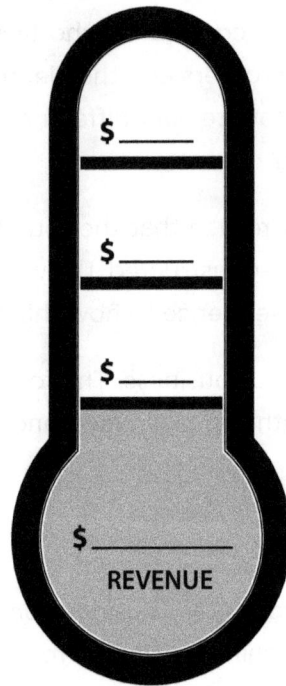

$_____

REVENUE

C.O.I. _____

These stages of business growth are applicable to almost all businesses, whether they are online, face-to-face, bricks and mortar, or product-based. Although you'll notice that the activities are primarily for service-based businesses, the stages are still applicable to retailers, consultants, authors, speakers and other professionals such as financial advisors, real estate professionals, etc. Let's review the stages.

Stage 1: GLORIFIED EMPLOYEE

For many of you, this stage may seem to take forever! It starts with your original business dream and then heads into testing it in the marketplace to see if you have a viable product (yes, your solution is the product).

Primary Foci:

- Client creation (sales and marketing)
- Development of Consistent Minimum Fixed Income (CMFI) to cover fixed expenses
- Building of **10 Foundational Biz Must-Haves** (See Chapter 4 – A Poor Foundation)

If you spend most of your time and mental energy creating clients and just trying to cover expenses, then there's a pretty good chance you're at Stage 1. I call this the Glorified Employee stage because, in fact, it seems as though you have just created a job for yourself. You work long, hard hours and there's little of the time freedom that you thought there would be.

Other Characteristics of This Stage:

- Sales are coming in but cash flow is a rollercoaster
- You wear all the hats because there is no budget to hire out
- A tremendous amount of your time is spent in learning curves!

Suggested Activities:

- Build a solid foundation on which to grow your business (Download my **10 Foundational Biz Must-Haves** at www.dianalidstone.com/bookresources).
- Sell one-on-one coaching/programs/consultations (it's easier to sell one-on-one – it's only one sale and your list/network/tribe isn't that big!).
- Create products/programs that give you Consistent Minimum Fixed Income (CMFI) to cover your basic expenses (i.e. Done-for-You services, rolling group programs where clients can join at any time since there is no fixed start date, maintenance programs). For some of you, CMFI may come from your family savings, your spouse's income, a loan, or a full or part-time job..

Common Mistakes:

- Dabbling in other stages when you haven't covered your costs (i.e. large group programs, writing a book, online programs)
- Spending a HUGE amount of time going to networking events without ever booking discovery or sales calls
- Spending large amounts of time on social media without developing relationships further towards having a sales conversation

What NOT to FOCUS on:

- Webinars (paid)
- Joint ventures
- Hosting large live events
- Hiring staff (other than eventually a bookkeeper)
- Marketing automation
- Paid social media
- Guest blogging
- Expensive websites

Remember: you don't go to bed one night in the Glorified Employee stage and wake up the next morning in the Manager stage! It's a process and it happens gradually, like the workings of a thermometer!

Stage 2: MANAGER

You know you're in the Manager Stage when:

- Client creation is running well — and it's automated (your list is growing slowly)
- You've figured out your best marketing methods (speaking, networking, etc.)
- Basic business systems are in place (CRM, autoresponders, calendar)
- Expenses are well covered by your Consistent Minimum Fixed Income (CMFI). In fact, profit may be at an all-time high
- Amongst completed activities are market research, a basic website and several social media profiles.
- Your *Detailed Dream* is clear, you have clarity on the problem that you solve, and you have several simple one-on-one program offerings (proposals, retainers, etc.)
- Your calendar is bursting at the seams with one-on-one clients
- You are making great money but you don't have the time to enjoy it

Primary Foci:

- Leveraging your time with group programs; selling one-to-many; using interns or other coaches
- Delegating administrative duties to an assistant or specialized individuals (i.e. social media, technical support, etc.)
- Developing systems for future growth, i.e. standard operating procedures for hiring; development of email list automation

Suggested Activities:

- **Leveraging** by creating group programs (every business can do this – for example you could host webinars that cover your most common FAQs, such as market updates for a financial advisor or real estate team; you can create consistent online content with guest interviews; speak one-to-many)

- **Delegating** – This is often the most difficult stage for many small business owners. They are used to doing everything themselves and now it's time to make a shift to delegating and hiring superstars. Hopefully by this stage you already have a bookkeeper, now is a good time to find someone to help with administrative tasks that you don't like doing (verifying appointments, social media, content creation, etc.) As your business grows, you increased your team members.
- **Systems** creation by focusing on conscious big list building efforts, etc. (Moving from 1,000 to 10,000 email addresses); instituting Standard Operating Procedures (SOPs); adding specialized online systems; contact management systems; etc.

Common Mistakes:

- Building online programs such as membership programs without having a sufficient email list... that's when the struggle and frustration comes in. So this is a case of a business owner playing at the Manager level – when they are truly only an Glorified Employee.
- Hiring/firing mistakes if there aren't standard operating procedures in place or a clear vision for the new employee

What NOT to FOCUS on:

- Joint ventures
- Large speaking events
- One-on-one client programs

Stage 3: CEO

You know you are at the CEO stage when:

• Your time is well leveraged and a large portion of your income comes from scalable income
• You spend your time doing the things that you are really good at
• Your systems are well in place and your contact/email list is growing substantially
• You are creating serious money (prosperity) – those days of feeling penniless seem so far away
• You have the time to enjoy your money

Few business owners actually reach this level of success.

Primary Foci:

• Expanding your reach in bigger ways, perhaps globally
• Developing corporate and self-leadership programs
• Building a bigger team

Suggested Activities:

• Creating a corporate culture that attracts superstar employees into your business.
• Get out there in a bigger way – multiple three-day events, big book launches, speaking to large audiences, media interviews, etc.
• Build a bigger team with specialized individuals (remember, you used to do it all yourself? Not now!) A coach at this level might have some other coaches working for them who are leading some group programs; a real estate team would be growing to several individuals; your email list is growing towards, or surpassing, the 100,000 mark.

Common Mistakes:

• If you're still scrambling to pay the expenses, and get clients, and you are out attempting to hire staff; OR trying to get your presence known in a really big way such as with big three-day live events; OR you are spending time and money on a best-selling book; OR you are trying to fill online courses with big numbers – then it sounds like you're doing the wrong things at the wrong time. It sounds like you're playing at the CEO level but you're really only a Glorified Employee.

• The reverse is also true .... I see business owners who truly are at the CEO level but they are dabbling in activities at the Glorified Employee level instead of building their leadership skills and leading a bigger team. So although their business revenue might be big – they are still focused on Glorified Employee level activities.

What NOT to FOCUS on:

• Administrative duties
• Client creation or marketing
• Any activity that a team member could/should be doing

Stage 4: LEGACY

At this stage in your growth everything is in play and running smoothly –

- Clients are coming in almost automatically
- Systems are automated and running smoothly
- Business now runs without your daily input
- You focus only on the things that you love to do
- Your list is continuously growing
- You're out there in a bigger way
- You have a company culture
- You are making the kind of money you always wanted and you have the freedom you were seeking.

Primary Foci:

- Maintaining market position; keeping an eye on the competition
- Developing an exit strategy; establishing a legacy/movement
- Building diversity or acquiring other businesses that support yours

Suggested Activities:

- Keep your eyes on the competition and upstarts who may challenge your position
- Invest in developing the leaders in your business
- Diversification...Here's an example: a rather famous coach in the US went from five-figure debt to a multi-million dollar business in less than 10 years. She hired coaches to help her coach, she put on live events—each of which was bigger and better than the previous one—she wrote a best seller, she developed an event company, and she built a video company. And more.

Common Mistakes:

- If you are thinking about expanding your team in a big way, or you are thinking about diversifying your business BUT you are still trying to pay your bills then you're spending your time on the wrong activities.

What NOT to FOCUS on:

- Administrative duties
- Client creation and marketing

It probably seems as though you'll never reach Legacy stage—right? But perhaps that's not your goal in life.

What it's costing you?

Are you clear on your current stage of business growth? Have you identified your stage?

Take the time to get clear before you continue or the following exercise won't make much sense.

Perhaps you noticed but we haven't talked about money yet with respect to the stages of business growth. That's okay because it is really important to focus first on the activities, not the money. Now it's time to talk money.

You'll notice on the *Grow-Meter*™ that there are dollar signs and a line next to each stage of business growth. Here's a little exercise that will point out what it is costing you to focus on activities that are not appropriate for your stage of business growth.

EXERCISE:

1. Beside your current stage of business growth, write the amount of money your business pays you each month on a consistent basis. Are you making $2,000; $5,000 or $20,000 per month regularly. Now be sure to be honest. This isn't meant to reflect that one month you earn $10,000 and another month you earn $1,000.

What's your number? _____

2. Now go to the stage of business growth ABOVE where you are currently. So if you are currently a Glorified Employee, look at the Manager level.

   Explanation: Over the years, I've tested these figures and they play out consistently for service-based businesses. For our calculations, we are going to use $5,000 per month.

   - As a **Glorified Employee**, owners typically earn approximately $5-7,000 per month.
   - A **Manager** typically earns twice or $5,000 x 2 = $10,000 per month
   - A **CEO** typically earns four times or $10,000 x 4 = $40,000 per month
   - At **Legacy**, owners typically earn ten times or $40,000 x 10 = $400,000 per month.

In the stage above you, write the typical income number.
So if you are a Glorified Employee, write on the Manager level $10,000
If you are a Manager, write on the CEO level $40,000

3. You should now have 2 numbers on your *Grow-Meter*™; one large and one smaller.

4. Subtract the two numbers and place that number on the C.O.I. line.
   $10,000 minus $5,000 = $5,000 that you write on the C.O.I line.

5. The COI line is your **Cost of Inaction**! That is your cost of staying stuck at this level, month after month, year after year.

Now – let's reduce your C.O.I. and get into the right kind of action for your stage of business growth!

ROADBLOCK #2: Shifting Actions

1. What stage are you at now in your business?

_____

_____

2. What stage do you believe you will have attained in three years from now?

_____

_____

3. Which activities should you be focusing on?

_____

_____

4. Which activities should you omit?

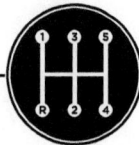

_____

_____

ROADBLOCK #3: Wandering Aimlessly

I've discovered that there is a disease which runs rampant amongst small business owners. It's difficult to cure but it's quite easy to diagnose. There is no magic pill to cure it. It takes commitment to ensure that you move past it. Perhaps you've seen it out there? It's known as BSOS, or bright shiny object syndrome. It occurs when a small business owner scurries like an obsessed squirrel from one activity to another, never really getting one activity correct before moving on to the next. The squirrel has no plan of action; he is distracted by every bright shiny object that comes along.

ROADBLOCK #3: Too many small business owners don't have a plan, a strategy, as to HOW they are going to make money and profit. You don't reach Successville by accident.

Wandering aimlessly, going from one unplanned activity to another, is not how you get rich! No successful entrepreneur has ever made millions without a plan, a road map or a strategy! It's time to figure out how you are going to get to Successville

Before we 'build' your money-making plan, though, let's consider these important points:

1. To get different results, you have to be ready to start doing things differently than you have in the past. Einstein's definition of crazy was the act of doing the same things over and over again and expecting different results. What I know for sure is that you can build a wonderful money-

making plan, but if you aren't ready to change, and do things differently, no plan in the world is going to work. Ask yourself this: are you ready to change?

2. Stress-free money making comes from having a plan that allows you to know exactly when you've arrived at Successville. In other words, every plan requires milestones and some units of measurement to monitor your progress. That means you need to be comfortable talking about your money as well as the other indicators you'll need to measure (more on that later).

3. Plans are not tattoos – they change more often than you think. That's a good thing! I recommend creating a 90-day plan. At the end of 90 days review and re-evaluate, what has worked and what hasn't. Make some adjustments. If it's working, how can you do more of it? If it's not working, consider how to improve, or do less.

4. Focus on the right activities for your level of business growth (See my *Grow-Meter*™ in Chapter 2). If you are at the Glorified Employee level, don't worry about writing a book, doing paid social media ads or hosting paid webinars!

5. Ensure that you have the 10 Foundational Biz Must Haves (Chapter 4) in place, and master them before spending your focus elsewhere. You're building a foundation for growth.

6. Consistent results come from consistent actions. You've probably got the hint by now that "commitment" and "focus" are two qualities that will drive your success. When your passion is aligned, then commitment and focus will be easy.

7. You are the leader of your business. That means that you don't have a leader; you are the leader! Shifting into being a leader might be your most difficult transformation. As women, most of us come from places where we were not the leader. In school, there's a teacher. In college, there's a professor. In the corporate world, there's a boss. SHIFT – you are the leader, even if you don't have employees, because some day you will have a team. You'll have a bookkeeper, a

financial advisor, a house keeper, an assistant, and an intern. Business Strategist Tara Gentile calls this "self-leadership." It's about making decisions. Big bold choices will move your business forward. You are going to need a team of some sort – no successful person built a business by themselves!

Why Do You Need a Money-Making Plan?

I know that many business owners feel that a plan is a four-letter word! They hate it! They think that a plan is too constricting and doesn't allow for a creative process. They think that a plan takes too much time to create, and who follows it anyway? They think that a plan isn't the way to go. But here's the thing: without a plan, road map or strategy:

• You'll never know what your next move will be
• You won't know how to prioritize your actions
• You won't know what to do with all the information that you do have
• You won't have time for the things or people you love
• You'll continue to suffer from BSOS
• Your journey to Successville will cost you more money, time and energy than necessary!

Successful, profitable businesses (even micro businesses) have a plan. You need one!

A stress-free profit plan has four basic stages: Dream It; Believe It; Plan It; Do It.

Dream It

Step 1   Starting Point (Nowville)

Step 2   Rear view mirror analysis

Step 3   Your Three-Year Destination (Successville)

Believe It

Step 4   Believe Bigger – Leap

Plan It

Step 5   Quantifying Successville: Three-year milestones

Step 6   Quantify Annual Milestones

Step 7   Develop and Price Programs/Products to Sell

Step 8   Decide and Schedule Your Preferred Marketing Methods

Step 9   Quantify Quarterly Milestones

Step 10   Quantify Monthly Milestones

Step 11   Quantify Weekly and Daily Milestones

Do It

Step 12   Schedule it

Step 13   Anticipate, Measure, Monitor, Adjust

A PROFIT PLAN isn't your father's business plan!

A profit plan is a stress-free money-making plan which includes your:
• Marketing plan
• Program/product launch plan
• Employee hiring/firing plan
• Purchasing, budgeting and cash flow plans
• Monitoring of key indicators and milestones, and
• Action steps to take you to your destination

A profit plan is NOT a business plan. Typical business plans are static and typically they are generally created for financial institutions so that you can apply for loans or funding. A profit plan is a living breathing process–and it's for you, not some other institution. It also:

• Takes time to build
• Is not set in stone
• Must be reviewed regularly and adjusted
• Must be kept in plain sight and worked on daily!
• Represents your ROAD MAP, so that you know what to do, and so that you feel confident doing it!

Before I opened my retail store, my team and I created a business plan for the bank in order to get some necessary funding. I continued to plan each year, but I wasn't creating more business plans – I was making plans that set out our direction and our focus. We needed plans so that we could achieve our vision. Our plans laid out what type of products we would purchase, what our budgets were, how much profit we would make and when we would hire additional staff.

 Probably around year three, I realized that I couldn't create a plan while at the store or at my home. There were always interruptions – clients, sales reps, employees, kids, pets, etc. If there weren't interruptions, then there were distractions – laundry, inventory that had to be returned, etc. So my husband and I decided that we would schedule a couple of days away from the madding crowd twice a year before our buying trips. Not only was it great to get away with my hubby, but we found that we could be creative in the new surroundings. We could talk without interruption. We could brainstorm. We could think outside the box. We got a lot accomplished and we always came back feeling renewed and confident that we were going in the right direction. It was a wonderful feeling. Building your profit plan can be fun.

What is Profit and Why Should You Care?

Business has money coming in (revenue, sales) and money going out (expenses). I'm assuming that you want to keep some of that money for yourself to fund your desired lifestyle. PROFIT is the money left over after expenses that your business pays you. Your business might pay you dividends or fund your family vacation, or it might fund your retirement. Profit is the money that your business gives you so that you can live the life you want!

The first rule of profit:
your labour and your salary are NOT profit!
They are expenses!

Your business is meant to fund your lifestyle! If you aren't being paid on a regular and consistent basis by your business, then your business isn't doing its job! During an initial conversation with Nora, a prospective client, she told me about her photography business. She noted that she worked every weekend photographing weddings, and the only way she could make more money was by hiring another photographer. My initial thought was that she must be doing well. Very well.

However, the more I listened, the more I realized that Nora was dealing with a number of problems that are quite common among small business owners:

1. Nora had no idea how much money she was making because she just bundled up all of her receipts at the end of the year and gave them to her accountant for tax purposes. She wasn't measuring what mattered, and she had no plan for creating consistent profit.

2. Nora had no idea how much profit she was making per wedding shoot. She didn't know the cost of creation, the cost of delivery or the cost of her overhead.

3. Nora's business didn't pay her regularly. She took out occasional money for training, equipment and groceries.

4. Nora had trouble making wise business decisions because she didn't know her numbers.

5. Nora didn't have a plan to strategically grow her business, and she was overwhelmed and stressed! She was just working to pay her bills!

Nora needed help to create a strategic Profit Plan that would help her understand her sales, her revenue and her profit margins, and allow her to spend time with her young family! She needed a plan so that she could stop working endless hours and yet put more money in her pocket. Recognizing the challenges she was facing, and anxious about resolving them, Nora immediately booked time with me. We created her stress-free money making plan, and found a system that allowed her to easily track her money flow. She discovered that she could increase her prices by creating added value that cost her very little. She left our session feeling a lot more confident about her future business growth!

A Planning Process

If you've been doing the exercises in this book, you've already completed a good portion of your Profit Plan. Congratulations! Let's examine the third section of the plan: **Plan It**. This is the section where you have to quantify your success by working backwards.

An example might be:

Your Successville in three years = $400,000 revenue

Your Successville in two years = $300,000 revenue

Your Successville in one year = $200,000 revenue

1st Quarter = $75,000	Why?	Big program/product launch
2nd Quarter = $45,000	Why?	
3rd Quarter = $45,000	Why?	Summer vacation
4th Quarter = $35,000	Why?	Time off for holidays

Feel free to download several easy-to-use templates at www.dianalidstone. com/bookresources. There's one you can use for your annual revenue and another for your 90-day success plan. Use them over and over again as you adjust your plan.

A Word About Programs Versus Packages:

If you are building a service-based business, such as a coaching business, it's imperative to realize the difference between programs and packages. The difference affects your profits substantially! (Note: a consulting business would probably work by retainers, proposals or contracts).

Let's use the example of a fitness trainer or coach. It's common for these professionals to charge by the hour and sell packages, i.e. buy 10 hours of training for the price of eight. However that means that the fitness trainer is trading dollars for hours. It's a common model, but one that doesn't lead to shifting into rich!

An improved pricing structure would be to offer a "program." A program is perceived as having higher value. A fitness program might be Six Months To Skinny Jeans where the client pays a regular monthly fee (for six months) and receives not only fitness coaching, but also healthy eating coaching, a recipe book, etc. Value, value, value! A program such as this is perceived by a client as being far more valuable than just a package of 10 classes for the price of eight classes. More value, more profit!

How Many Programs/Products Do You Need?

Here's where the planning and number-crunching really takes place. It's time to calculate how many of each program you need to sell in order to reach your the milestone targets that you set earlier. How many in each month? Each quarter? Each year? Once you know how many you need to sell, it's a matter of doing the marketing to generate the sales. (We'll explore marketing and sales in Chapter 5.)

ROADBLOCK #3: Shifting Actions

1. Download the available templates and tools to build your Profit Plan (www.dianalidstone.com/bookresources).

2. Create a folder on your computer or create a binder with all the elements of your Profit Plan, including your *Detailed Dream*, etc. (I like calling this your Driver's Manual).

3. Start putting numbers into your plan. Start with the big picture (three years) and then reverse engineer right down to the month, week or day!

4. Join the **Achiever's Club** (www.dianalidstone.com/achieversclub) for a supportive community to hold you accountable; to hang around others who are striving towards Successville; and to learn from other experts in the group.

We've explored the "route" for your journey to Successville. Now we are ready to step into the next area that's stopping you from shifting into rich. We are going to talk about the actual car you are going to drive — its framework or foundation, the fuel it needs and its gauges.!

Section 2
Your Car

ROADBLOCK #4: A Poor Foundation

Much like your house needs a strong, square foundation, and your car needs to run on good tires and have a strong chassis, your business also needs a good foundation on which to grow. Over the years, I've noticed that many small business owners focus not only on the wrong activities at the wrong time, but they forget to implement the basic foundational elements that allow a business to thrive and to be poised for future growth. Instead, I see them worrying about whether their tagline sounds perfect, whether their website has great search engine optimization, or whether their business cards are stunning.

ROADBLOCK #4: There is a sequence to building a successful business and it starts by building a strong foundation for future growth.

Here's what I've learned—the hard way—over the years: you'll change your business cards several times as you and your business grow and mature. You can't possibly create a perfect tag line when you first start out because really you are still in testing mode. You'll also have your website redone a few times before you get it right. So give yourself a break.

Here are three pieces of advice I give all my clients:

1. Done is better than none. In other words don't get stuck in analysis paralysis. It doesn't need to be perfect!

2. Take care of yourself every day, and mind your health. As the leader of your company, you need to be the best you possible. Exercise, eat right, meditate, journal, and tend to your mindset.

3. Have sales conversations with prospects, either clients or past clients, every day. Make it your goal to connect with at least five people daily and ask how you can help them.

That's it! Every day, you only need to focus on those three activities! So why the overwhelm? Why the confusion? Why do you feel that you have to do it all? It's not your fault. I know that every single day you are bombarded with one expert after another telling you that you need to improve your LinkedIn, to use the latest social media platform like Facebook, Instagram, Periscope, Facebook Live, etc. The list goes on and on. Believe me, you don't need it all at once. I know plenty of individuals who have built very successful businesses with a one-page website, or with a simple business card that has only their contact information on it, or with only one marketing method! You can, too!

Three things every day...Done is better than none, take care of yourself, have a sales conversation. It seems to me that if you start the morning with those three things in mind, then that should take you to about 10:00 a.m., or maybe 11:00 a.m. What do you do the rest of the day? Work with clients, create clients and build your foundation so you are poised for future growth!

What Does Your Business Foundation Look Like?

When you start off in your business, at the Glorified Employee stage, there are only 10 things you really need to put into place, and they don't have to be perfect! See the checklist of **10 Foundational Biz Must-Haves**.

I'd like to walk you through an exercise that I do with each client. Read down the list of the **10 Foundational Biz Must-Haves**. If you have not done one of these elements, or your current version needs updating, or improving, then put a checkmark in the "Need To Do" column. If you have been doing the exercises as we go along in the book, then you've already completed #1. And you worked on #2. If you already have a coach, then #10 is also complete. Well done!

I can almost hear you saying..."OMG, there's so much to do!" Yes there is, especially at the Glorified Employee stage. At this stage, there's a huge learning curve. You have a choice: either pay someone to do it for you OR learn how to do it yourself! Most people don't have the resources early in their business to pay someone, so there's lots of time spent learning! That's why I developed my group coaching program—to shorten the learning curve and to help you avoid mistakes the first time around. Members of this program receive webinar recordings and workbooks for each of these **10 Foundational Biz Must-Haves** to substantially enhance the process and eliminate their roadblocks to success!

Stage 1- 10 Foundational Biz Must-Haves

NEED TO DO	ESSENTIAL Foundational Biz 'Must-Haves'
	1. Create a Detailed Dream for your business and how it supports your desired lifestyle.
	2. Cultivate a positive Money Mindset. (Master Your Money Game)
	3. Know what problems you solve and for whom.(Master Your Dream Client)
	4. Develop a compelling marketing message. (Master Your Message)
	5. Build, follow and adjust your Profit Plan. (Master Your Profit Plan)
	6. Create specific paid programs (solutions) which are appropriate to your stage of business (Master Your Money Mountain).
	7. Launch a basic website with an opt-in that gives people a sizzling lead magnet creating a list of prospects that you can nurture into clients (Master Your Basic Website).
	8. Activate simple, cost-effective office systems including an autoresponder such as Mail Chimp; a CRM such as TealCRM or Less Annoying; & a scheduler (Master Your Office Systems).
	9. Create a Simplified Marketing Schedule that you follow on a consistent basis to reach your desired results. (Master Your Marketing)
	10. Hire A coach/mentor to support you; to believe in you; who knows you are capable of playing BIGGER; (Master Your Success).

Let's briefly review each of these **10 Foundational Biz Must-Haves**:

1. **Create your vision.** Write your *Detailed Dream* for your business and how it supports your desired lifestyle.

2. **Cultivate a positive Money Mindset.** Just a reminder that this is ongoing work! As you progress up the *Grow-Meter*™, you'll encounter a bigger money monster and may need to do more inner work to tame it!

3. **Know what problems you solve and for whom.** Businesses exists because people pay to get their problems solved or to achieve a clear result! They pay to travel from Point A to Point B, whether it's in a car, bus, train or plane. They pay to have food, whether it's fast food or from a grocery store. They pay to have shelter, whether it's a luxury condo or a three-bedroom family home. An interesting exercise is to watch television commercials and try to figure out what problem or result each commercial is aimed at satisfying!

Your prospects have to be able to clearly understand what their problem is, and what your solution to that problem is. It's not a simple process, because most small business owners want to help everyone. They want to solve everyone's problem. However, I'm sure you've heard it before...If you try selling to everyone, you sell to no one! Sage advice is to focus on becoming known as an expert for solving one problem, then people will come to you to solve other problems as well! When you figure out your answer to this key foundational element, your marketing is almost done!

A great example of this comes from a friend of mine, Sue-Anne Hickey, who was working to grow her naturopathic business in Montreal. There are many naturopaths who all solve similar health problems. But she wondered how she could stand out from all of the others; how she could be perceived as different. Sue-Anne struggled with this problem until she hired a coach who helped her create her signature weight loss program based on body type and shape (bodytypology.com). It wasn't long before her practice was full. She became known as the weight loss expert! Once people trusted her for solving that problem, they came to her to solve other problems!

The same was true of a client of mine, Frankie, who was a great "technical" expert. She could build websites, social media platforms, and help any small business with online issues. However, that wasn't bringing her a steady flow of customers because she wasn't perceived as 'different' from the other technical experts. After deciding to become positioned as a LinkedIn expert, clients started coming to her for LinkedIn assistance and they were so pleased with her work that they also hired her for other social media platforms. She became known as "the LinkedIn expert" and she was easy to refer!

Pick a lane and become a known expert for just one thing!
Diana Lidstone

4. **Develop a compelling marketing message.** If you can't explain to your prospects what you do, who will explain it for you? All of your marketing (Facebook, networking, speaking, etc.) must be focused around a message that answers: **So what do you do?**

   In their minds, your prospects are really asking:

   • What do you do that interests me?
   • Why should I listen to you?
   • Will it work for me?

   My clients work through a process that gets your dream prospects saying..."Oh my God, I want to work with you!"

5. **Build, follow and adjust your Profit Plan.** You will notice that I call this a PROFIT plan. It's not a sales plan; it's not a revenue plan. It's a plan that shows you where and how the money is coming into your business and where it's going out! I laugh occasionally when people tell me about their six or seven figure business! It doesn't matter to your lifestyle or

to your family that your sales are six or seven figures. What's important is how much money you have left over to spend on your family and lifestyle! Isn't that why you got into business?

6. **Create specific paid programs/products.** We've already discussed the different stages of business growth (*Grow-Meter*™) and we noted that there were certain activities appropriate to each level of growth. For instance, paid webinars might not be appropriate for you in the Employee stage, but once you have sufficient following/tribe/email list, they would be profitable!

No one ever became a millionaire by getting paid by the hour. Service-based, small businesses very often offer packages, i.e. fitness clubs. This is still being paid by the hour. Programs, however, are not based on an hourly wage but on the value they deliver! If you have a product-based business, you won't make millions by selling the products by yourself; you will need distributors or sales people (who are not needed in the first stage of business growth).

It's also important to have a MONEY MOUNTAIN for your business. This is especially true if your business has an online element. A MONEY MOUNTAIN is based on gathering prospects' information at the FREE level and then working them up to the top of the mountain.

A business coach's money mountain might look like this:

- FREE might include free checklists, speaking, discovery calls or consultations
- Offer a webinar ($97) that solves people's most immediate problem
- Offer $397 workshop
- Offer $697 monthly mastermind program
- Offer one-on-one coaching
- Offer a warm weather business get-away

Each of these offers is increasingly costly as you move up the Money Mountain—as you increase your Know-Like-Trust factor.

7. **Launch a simple website.** I emphasize the word SIMPLE and advise people to ensure they have a sizzling lead magnet (opt-in). Yes, every single business needs to gather email contact information by having at least one sizzling lead magnet. It doesn't matter if you're a real estate agent, an interior designer, a massage therapist or you sell widgets! Capturing email addresses is how you keep in touch with prospects; it's how you nurture prospects into clients. I've had individuals on my email list for two years before they were in a position to hire me! (P.S. Make sure that your telephone number is easy for your customers to find on your website!)

8. **Activate simple, cost-effective office systems.** When you are in the first phase of growth, FREE is good. There are wonderful FREE tools such as MailChimp, PicMonkey, TealCRM and many others that are very low cost and help keep you organized. If you want to build a business that is poised for future growth, you will need systems!

   I remember when we were planning to open our retail store in 1995. It was almost unheard-of for a stand-alone store like ours to have a computerized point-of-sale system to manage inventory and pricing! However, we delayed our opening until we could get our computer system up and running. We were poised for growth. Poised so we could analyze our inventory turnaround and our profit margins. It's what allowed us to make good decisions and be profitable!

9. **Follow a simplified marketing system.** Marketing shouldn't be complicated or overwhelming. I teach clients that there are probably only four-to-six marketing methods that are true money-making activities. In your early stages, you'll discover which ones work best for you. It took me a while to find out that my preferred method is speaking. You'll find your strength and then you'll want to do more of it. For each of my clients, we work out their initial marketing schedule and I ask them to commit to it.

In the Glorified Employee stage, it might look something like this:

Post on ONE social media platform	3x/week and work up to 5 x/week
Post on a 2nd social media platform	As you become more advanced
Sales Conversations	At least 1x/week; later at least 3-5x/week
Blog/Newsletter	Start with 2x/month; work up to 4x/month
Networking	1x/week; later 2x/week
Speaking/Seminars	1x/month; work up to 2x/month
Webinars	1x/90 days; later 1x/45 days
Sponsorships	1x/90 days; later 1x/45 days

Consistent Commitment = Consistent Results

Diana Lidstone

10. **Hire a Coach.** No successful person built their business by themselves! No one! It doesn't matter if you are Oprah Winfrey, Jack Canfield, an Olympian, or a New York Times Best Selling author, none of them started out successful. All of them had a mentor or a coach. All of them built a team.

So why do so many small business owners think they can do it by themselves? I think I've heard almost every excuse and that's okay! I'm not judging you. If you are like me, your inner critic or your money monster might be screaming things like:

- I don't have the money sitting in my bank account right now (Like, who does?!)
- It's such a big investment (Aren't you worth it? Do your clients think you are worth it?)
- It's not the right time now (Trust me, it's never going to be the perfect time!)

I remember when I hired my first coach. I didn't have the money sitting in my bank account. I worked out a payment plan. I scrounged and saved; and I made a commitment to grow my business. And grow it did: from a few hundred dollars a month to thousands of dollars a month. Could I have done it on my own? Unlikely that I would have pushed myself; unlikely that I would have seen the bigger vision for my business myself; unlikely that I would have worked on my personal growth. Just remember - it's really hard to give yourself a good hair cut! Find a coach who has walked the path before you, one with whom you feel comfortable sharing your deepest secrets. And go for it!. It's the best investment you'll make in your business!

ROADBLOCK #4: Shifting Actions

1. Complete the exercise to identify which of the
   10 Foundational Biz Must-Haves you don't have in place.

2. Prioritize the ones you need to implement.

3. Work to complete all 10 so that you are poised for growth.

4. Remember to focus on three main activities daily (done is better than none, self-care and sales)

5. Give yourself permission to ask for help.

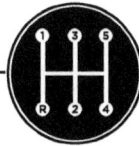

So those are the "tires" on your car! The foundation on which to build profitable growth. The next thing you need on your journey is a plan for how you will turn your vision into reality.

ROADBLOCK #5: The Incorrect Fuel

Marketing is to your business as gas is to your car. It gives your business engine the necessary "fuel" to move forward. Marketing fuels your sales. Marketing creates leads and prospects. Marketing starts the conversation that leads to building relationships that create clients. Without clients, well, you just don't have a business!

It's been my experience that most small business owners are totally overwhelmed by the choices of marketing methods available to them. There's social media (do I have to learn all of them?); there's networking (where do I go?); and webinars, book writing, email marketing, blogging, videos...and the list goes on. Experts in social media tell you that you have to run paid Facebook ads. Experts in search engine optimization (SEO) tell you that you need to spend money on SEO. Webinar experts promise that you'll grow your business with webinars! It's hard to know where to start and what to do.

ROADBLOCK #5: All marketing methods can be successful and all marketing methods can fail. It's not the method; it's the message in the method. To be a successful business owner, you must be crystal clear on WHAT you are marketing and to WHOM.

So what happens to a confused business owner when faced with this buffet of marketing? I usually see one of two things. I see a group of business owners who flit from one marketing method to another (BSOS - Squirrel!), spending a little time learning one method and when they feel it isn't working they skip on to the next method. Then there's the other group, who are like deer in the headlights: frozen. Frozen and doing nothing! I totally understand! You aren't alone. Marketing/fuel becomes a roadblock.

Simplified Marketing: The Top Six Marketing Methods

Whether your business is online or offline, there are six proven marketing methods that consistently lead to sales conversations. When you are just starting out as that Glorified Employee, focus on just one of these methods and get really good at it. Along the way, as you experiment, you'll most likely discover that one of these methods suits you, makes you happy, is easier for you and gives you better results. That will become your preferred method; that is the method to master!

1. SPONSORSHIPS

Be a paid sponsor at events that have the same (or similar) ideal target market as you, who have different problems for you to solve. For example, when I host my own live events for women entrepreneurs, I invite other businesses who also serve women entrepreneurs to sponsor the event. These might include insurance agents, health coaches, or retirement coaches. They all serve women but they offer a different product or service than I do.

Being a paid sponsor at an event isn't about getting people as clients right there on the spot but it's about starting a relationship with them, getting them on your email/contact list and then nurturing them. It's often scary, but it lets you be seen. Are you prepared to be seen as the expert in your field? The key to a successful sponsorship is about being prepared, and following up effectively.

Being a sponsor is an investment, just like any other form of marketing. So be wise as to which events you sponsor. Note how much each one is costing you and how you can improve on each event. Keep track of how many clients you received through the event and how many prospects you added to your list. Remember, like all good investments, sometimes the payoff is down the road!

The first time I sponsored an event I was scared to death. But thinking of it as "positioning myself as THE expert," made all the difference. Each time I host an event, I encourage my new clients to take the leap and become a sponsor. They've all agreed: it was worth the effort.

2. REFERRAL PARTNERS

The best people to act as referral partners are, of course, those who have experienced your work. They love you. They love the work that you do and the results that you get! You may have lots of clients who love you, but creating a referral partnership is something else. Not everyone has a circle of influence that contains those people that you'll love to work with. It often takes time and trial and error, but when you find the golden egg, that perfect referral partner, it will be worth it. Use creative ideas to determine how you can help each other!!!

3. NETWORKING (face-to-face)

Many clients tell me that they hate networking because it just seems as though there are 10 of your competitors out there passing out their business cards. It's true: you'll- it's often see the same tribe at these business events.

Here are a few quick recommendations to get more from networking events:

1. Go with a goal in mind (i.e. to have another sales conversation, to find a referral partner, to find a lead for a speaking event, etc.)

2. Be sure that you are "fishing in the right pond." Ask yourself if the networking group contains your Dream Client, your "fish".

3. If networking isn't producing the results you want, stop and re-evaluate. Ask yourself if you need to improve your 60-second infomercial, change networking groups, or decrease or increase your networking frequency

Improving your networking skills is a huge topic. Enough to say you need to get out from behind your desk and be seen if you want to be hired!

4. TELESEMINARS/WEBINARS (speaking online)

Teleseminars, teleclasses, and webinars are virtual speaking events and they are a great place to experiment. Many small business owners don't get involved with them because they are afraid of the technology. Don't be! There are many "platforms" to use and all of them come with videos and tutorials on how to use them (if I can learn, I'm sure a smart woman like yourself can, too!)

Today's webinar platforms are easy to use and they are not expensive. It's like working in your PJ's. One of the huge benefits is that you can record these sessions and use them to add value to another program.

I remember one of my first webinars: I had 50 people registered and I thought OMG that's awesome! Then my coach said, "Well, usually about half of the registrants actually show up." A little dejected, I decided that was okay for my first webinar. Then the ultimate disaster happened. It turned out that THERE WAS A HOCKEY PLAYOFF game—a semi-final—at the same time as my webinar. I had half of half show up. But at least it was a start – it was practice for bigger and better things!

Start by offering a free webinar on topics with which you are really familiar. Choose a topic, create a sexy, results-based name, let people know well in advance that you're running it, and keep reminding them to register and attend!

5. NEWSLETTERS/BLOG

Newsletters and blogs are about keeping in touch with past clients and about nurturing prospects. It's about sharing a little of you on a regular basis so that prospects get to know, like and trust you. Most people get bogged down in analysis paralysis. The truth is that your newsletter or blog doesn't have to be a Pulitzer Prize winning efforts –Done is Better than None! Once I figured that out, it was so much easier to write weekly.

Remember that you are writing as if your Dream Client were sitting across the kitchen table from you!

Your newsletter can be viewed as the "glue between offline and online." Consistency is the key, and remember: it takes time to build relationships!

6. SPEAKING EVENTS (including workshops)

In 2012, I held my first workshop entitled: 7 Deadly Follow-Up Sins. I had five participants and charged $25 each for two hours and plus a workbook. Today, things are very different. I hold several live events a year for 100+ women; I still hold workshops for small groups and I speak at universities, women's groups and professional chapter meetings. The point is that it's important just to start. Start small with what you know, but think long term award-winning thoughts. It's about taking that first small step and building on your successes!

Speaking is now my preferred marketing method. It allows the audience to experience me in person. You position yourself as the expert in your field simply by speaking. I don't know of any business that couldn't improve their sales by speaking and giving the audience value.

Some suggestions for speaking:

• Partner with another organization that already has a list such as Rotary Clubs, business networking clubs, etc.
• Provide them with marketing material: write the copy, print the flyer.
• Be sure that your presentation includes some type of ASK (sell something)
• At the end of each presentation, prepare the audience for the next level.
• Don't re-invent the wheel each time you speak. Learn to create a signature speech that you can give in 20 minutes or two hours!

Those are the top six marketing methods that will generate leads for your sales conversations. But here's the issue with most marketing – it's not the method that's the key, it's about what is being said!

Should You Buy a Red Car or a Blue Car?

Either a red car or a blue car will take you from point A to point B. They both have four wheels, an engine, seats, etc. However, they could be very different. One could be a luxury sedan and a gas guzzler; the other could be a compact hybrid. But they both do the job.

Mary chooses a blue car to take her to Successville. She fills it with premium gasoline and her journey goes smoothly. She encounters very few roadblocks or detours. John purchases a red car and it sputters, chokes, and even dies once in a while. His trip seemed to take him forever. He seemed to find every roadblock and pothole. Now, John has been watching Mary and her blue car for quite some time. He notices how smoothly things are going for Mary. So he decides to change cars. He buys a blue car, just like Mary's. After a while, the blue car is acting just like John's old red car: it's sputtering, and coughing and, again, the trip isn't going well. John can't figure out why his new blue car isn't acting more like Mary's!

There's one small difference! Remember I said that Mary put premium gasoline in her car? John didn't want to take the time or to spend the money to put premium gasoline in either his new blue car or his old red car. He bought whatever was cheapest and easiest! It turns out that it wasn't the car (the marketing method) that was causing the problem, but what he was putting into it (the message) that caused his results!

The analogy is the same for your marketing. You can choose ANY marketing method and it will work. You can choose ANY marketing method and it won't work. It's what you put in it that counts. It's what the marketing message says that counts! Here's what I mean. I'm sure you've met people like Cynthia. One week she's working on creating Facebook ads to move her business forward because she took a free webinar from a FB ad expert. Then she hears from a LinkedIn expert who says that success can only come from LinkedIn. Or webinars, Periscope, speaking, networking, etc. I think you get the idea. Cynthia continues to try different marketing methods (different color cars) but it's what she's saying that's important (fuel). Any marketing method will work; any marketing method won't work!

What Kind of Fuel Will You Buy?

Let's take a step backwards for a moment. The first rule for creating clients is that people BUY to solve a problem or to get a specific result (they want some change or transformation). Whether it's to make more money, fit into their skinny jeans, find their soul-mate, etc. What problem do you solve? That's the fuel you put into your car: it's a key part of your marketing!

Business strategist, Tara Gentile, says that products and services can "create" change for your customers in one or more of six main ways. They can:

1. **Change Behaviour** by helping customers stop doing one thing and start doing another. For example, a meal delivery service helps you stop eating out so much and start eating more healthy food at home.

2. **Change Skills** by teaching clients or customers something new. *My Fast Cash Intensive*, for example, teaches you four steps to fast cash!

3. **Change your Environment** or circumstances. An interior designer might help you "turn a house into a home," for example.

4. **Change Your Mindset or Belief**. I've developed my Master *Your Money Monster* webinar to help people learn how to change their relationship with money.

5. **Change your Feelings.** A program on sales could help customers so that they don't feel pushy or "salesy."

6. **Change your Identity** to help your customers see themselves in a whole new way.

Your product or service might accomplish one of these things or several. Tara points out that it's usually easier to sell prospects on #1, #2, and #3 than on the last three reasons for change. The other notable detail is that items #1 through #3 above are generally lower-priced than the last three. You might ask why: the answer is because any change that is related to self and emotion is perceived as being of a higher value than other kinds of change!

Before deciding that a marketing method doesn't work, be sure that you are communicating clearly to help your clients do one or more of the above. Be sure that you are articulating the fact that you are solving a problem that they are willing to pay to get resolved.

How Much Time Should I Spend on Marketing?

The answer is ... it depends! First of all, it depends on what stage of business growth you are in. Are you in Stage 1 - Glorified Employee? Or are you a CEO?

If you are in Stage 1 of your business growth, your main efforts, time and money are spent covering costs and therefore the majority of your time should be spent on effective marketing, i.e. creating clients! That could require up to 80% or more of your time!

However by the time you are at Stage 3 (CEO), your marketing is probably automated and runs like a well-oiled machine. In fact, you may have a marketing team or experts on staff that do the majority of your day to day marketing tasks.

Secondly, there are always "marketing" initiatives on which you could be executing. I believe that every single day we each need to connect with a prospect, a client, a past client, a referral source or a strategic partner. Whether that means picking up the telephone, sending an email or having lunch, the fact remains that business is born from relationships. No matter what stage of business growth you are in, you need to keep creating and strengthening relationships.

ROADBLOCK #5: Shifting Action

1. What fuel are you putting into your blue car? What problem are you solving and what result or change are you creating?

2. Which marketing methods bring the majority of your clients? How can you do more of what works?

3. Which marketing methods don't help to create clients? How can you do less?

4. Depending on your Stage of Business Growth, monitor how much time you spend marketing (creating clients)?

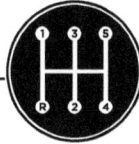

ROADBLOCK #6: Ignoring the Gauges

You're peacefully driving along and your car dashboard suddenly lights up and starts SCREAMING at you! "OMG," you wonder. "What's wrong?" You pull over to the side of the road and notice that it looks like there is smoke coming out from under the hood! You wonder if your car is going to burst into flames!

You call your local mechanic and he asks if there was any indication that this problem was coming. Did your temperature gauge run high? Did your oil light come on earlier? When was the last time you changed your oil? That's when you realize that you haven't been paying attention to your gauges.

It's the same for your business. There are key indicators that your business is successful or that you're headed for disaster. Are you paying attention to them? For many business owners, I believe that they think that this part of the business is too complicated so they either ignore the gauges or they give the responsibility away. There's a difference between delegating an activity, i.e. bookkeeping, and completely abdicating responsibility. Remember Nora, who only took her business receipts to her accountant at her year end? She was giving away her decision-making power. And she's not the only one.

ROADBLOCK #6: Many business owners don't pay enough attention to their numbers. Successful business owners measure what matters.

A client of mine, Georgina, hired a bookkeeper to do her monthly accounts. I was so proud of her because she was working to improve her delegation skills and get some of the daily tasks off her plate so that she could step up into being a great leader in her business. "Wonderful," I thought! Several months later, when we were discussing her profit margins and whether she needed to increase her prices, I asked her about her numbers: where was she sitting for the year-to-date; this year compared to the year before? And more. She didn't know! Her bookkeeper had not kept up the work on a monthly basis. She had given away her power and had no basis on which to make her decision about price increases. You can delegate many tasks, but it's still your responsibility to make sure the work is done in a timely manner!

Delegate don't abdicate!

Diana Lidstone

Why Are the Gauges Important?

In general, small business owners work really, really hard. I know that many of you work long hours, weekends, and overtime. However, if you aren't tracking your efforts, you often find yourselves working on things that aren't really generating sufficient revenue or profit. That's a waste of time and energy. And it's sad because I know that you didn't start your business to work longer and harder! So commit to monitoring your business gauges.

What's more, knowing your numbers gives you power: power to make the right decisions and take award-winning action! When you know that your profit is higher on one product over another, then you can make the decision to invest more in the more profitable product. Your choices are made on solid financial ground. And that's going to give you the lifestyle you want!

Which Gauges Are Important?

There are different categories of gauges in business, just like there are different types of gauges on your car dashboard. The most important are related to money, prospects, and customers.

The money-related gauges measure sales, profit, cash flow, bank balances, profit-per-product/program and customer life-time value (CLV).

The prospect-related gauges are based on your prospects and include the size of your email list, your social media reach, your web traffic, etc.

With respect to customers, it's important to monitor where your customers came from, how long they stayed, and the referrals sent to you.

For product-based businesses, inventory levels are extremely important to monitor. In some service-based businesses, you might also be monitoring customer satisfaction levels.

As your business grows, you will see how important it is to have systems in place to monitor your business gauges. That's why I teach clients to "think like a CEO." Start with the right systems in place so that you are poised for growth.

Remember that I mentioned earlier that my husband and I had delayed opening our retail store in order to ensure our computerized point-of-sale system was running properly? We wanted to be able to control our inventory and know precisely what was sold each day, and what the profit margin of each sold item was, etc. People thought we were crazy. I remember the first day the store was open: we were new to the POS system and it seemed to take forever to process a $5.00 sale of fudge. But it set us up the right way for the growth we knew was coming. It set us up for the growth we would experience selling $1,000 chairs and $4,000 orders of outdoor furniture!

Frequency of Monitoring Your Gauges:

SALES — I believe that you should be tracking your sales on a DAILY basis. In my retail store, not only did the computer track the daily sales, but the numbers were marked on a cheap calendar in the back office alongside our daily sales goal and the weather. Why weather? Because there are factors beyond our control that affect sales. In retail, weather can be a huge one. Another might be a political election or a traumatic global event.

If you have a service-based industry, tracking your sales is also important. You have to know that you are going to make more money than you spend. One great trick is to have a white board somewhere in your office so that you can track your sales, and prospective sales. When you see sales numbers daily, it keeps you focused on money-making activities!

For those of you just starting out, or those who don't have many sales transactions, you might find that a simple excel spreadsheet or a lined piece of paper will do just fine to for tracking what you want to earn each month, and to note which program/product it comes from.

CASH FLOW — Another important gauge for a business is cash flow and it needs constant monitoring. What is cash flow? Cash flow is all about the timing of the inflow and outflow of money. Having the cash on hand to pay for taxes—whether it's GST or income tax at the end of the year—is a big issue for many small business owners. This can be especially true for businesses with huge seasonal highs and lows like real estate, etc.

If your business doesn't have regular cash flow, you might consider creating some type of program/product offering that is paid monthly in order to keep cash flowing regularly. This could be a maintenance program or a done-for-you program. Every business can be creative and build regular, consistent income by having this type of product/program offering. Some examples:

• A real estate agent could create a property management business
• A pizza restaurant could create a membership club which special
  benefits for members including preferred parking for pick-up orders, etc.

- A social media expert/marketing expert could create a monthly done-for-you program that includes regular social media updates.
- A video company could create a monthly subscription package for video creation for coaches, authors and speakers.

With a little brainstorming and creativity, every business can create consistent monthly sales that cover basic monthly expenses!

If you aren't a good numbers person, or if you have trouble keeping up with your bookkeeping, I suggest getting a good resource person (accountant/bookkeeper) to help you keep ahead of the game. By budgeting and making cash flow predictions based on past performances and current trends your resource person can guide you to having enough cash on hand for your needs.

If you don't have a resource person, think like a CEO and get one – we'll talk more about building your team later. But you can start by creating your own cash flow spreadsheet.

NET PROFIT — I hear so many people talking about their sales or making six figures! However sales means absolutely nothing if you are spending as much as, or more than, you are making! The health of your biz is based on how much PROFIT you make, not on your sales.

For those of you who are interested ... check out a book entitled *Profit First*. The author, Mike Michalowicz, sets out "health check targets" and other general guidelines and it will help you get a good indication of where your money could be going.

Let's take a look at his recommendations for a small, service-based business with revenue is less than $250K. On my *Grow-Meter*™, this would be a business that is past the "Manager" stage and moving towards the "CEO" stage. I would consider these good targets to aim for:

Profit:	5%
Owner's pay (and/or Dividends):	50%
Tax (personal and coroporatecorporate):	15%
Operating Expenses:	30%

Profit Per Program/Product:

If you have a product-based business, what is your average profit per product? If you are selling a service, which of your services are most profitable?

CUSTOMER LIFE-TIME VALUE (CLV) — When considering how to invest in marketing, it's important to understand what your return on investment would be. If you invest $100 in social media marketing, and it nets you one new customer, that sounds great! However if your CLV is only $50, then investing $100 to get $50 is not a great investment. Consider if a customer comes to you and purchases a six-month group program, then they might up-level to private coaching or invest in several webinars. Start thinking customer life-time!

The CLV is also a great number to know if you are going to invest in yourself. For example, if you purchase an online program for $500, that immediately brings you three customers, and if each customer's LV is $1,000, then that's a $3,000 return. And a worthwhile investment!

EMAIL LIST SIZE — For those of you in the service industry (coaches, healers, and, yes, even professionals), your list is your inventory. It's your inventory of people you SUSPECT might do business with you in the future. They came to your website, they met you at an event, and they started the whole process of know-like-and-trusting you.

The truth is that they might not need your services today. In fact, Callan Rush, who teaches educational marketing, says that almost 60% of the people you meet won't need your services today, but they may down the road, or they will meet someone else who does need your services.

Starting a Beginner Email List

The easiest way to start your list is to use a free autoresponder such as MailChimp. Many business coaches advise that when you are just starting out you should add all of your family members and friends to your email list (yes, I know there are laws against adding people like that but these are your family and friends—if they don't want to be on your list, they will unsubscribe and I'm pretty sure they won't report you to the authorities).

Next, create a newsletter/blog and send it out – regularly! Don't forget to add yourself to the list as well.

When you are just starting out, another way of increasing a small list is to simply forward your newsletter to people who you've recently met, or who have purchased from you, and ask whether they would like to receive other timely information from you (I usually suggest that they "just hit reply and say YES!") Boom—they've been added!

By this time, your list should contain the names of a few hundred people. Aim to send your newsletter/blog out regularly at least once a month and eventually increase it to once a week. For those of you with an online business, and who want to dramatically build an email list, that's content for another book! However, eventually every business should have a sizzling lead magnet that is highly visible on their website.

If your local clothing store, grocery store and fast food res-taurant have an email list, then don't you think you should have one as well?

Diana Lidstone

In a recent conversation, a Montreal real estate agent who has been in the business for many years told me that not building her list was the BIGGEST mistake of her career. Don't wait to start!

Start your list and then build a marketing plan to grow your list and keep it well watered! Adding an opt-in box to your website could be one of the BEST investments you make in your business.

SOCIAL REACH — I will admit that I'm not a social media expert. But here are the basics. Social reach is your influence on social media. In other words, it revolves around your followers and their engagement with you, and the impact you have. Social media can be a huge part of a marketing plan because, ideally, you want to direct your Facebook friends and

LinkedIn followers to your website so that they become part of your email list and are "automatically" nurtured.

But here's the caution: social media shouldn't be considered a stand-alone marketing tool. It should be part of an overall "stacked," or integrated, marketing plan. One marketing method supports the others, and all of them present the same message.

Often I'm asked whether people need to be on social media and, if so, which ones are best. My reply is generally another question: where are your Dream Clients coming from right now? Perhaps it's speaking or perhaps it's your website or Yellow Pages ad. Master the marketing method that relates to wherever your clients are coming from!

Don't always assume that building a social media presence is the first thing you should be doing or that you should be on every social media platform! There are so many strategies today for marketing and I recommend starting with one; perfect it, and then add another strategy. Building a strong social media presence takes time, money and commitment.

Building a list and nurturing it could require another full day of learning but it's sufficient to say for our purposes today that you need to monitor and track it.

I encourage you to run your award-winning business like a CEO: be professional and know your numbers. It's your responsibility to monitor these numbers, but you can delegate the measuring or tracking.

Saving the Best for Last!

There are two gauges that I haven't talked about yet: **sales conversations and sales conversion rates**. These are the two gauges that many, many business owners don't monitor or track. You only have a business if you have sales! In order to have sales, you need to have sales conversations. You need to monitor how many sales conversations you have, and you need to know how many sales conversations it takes to convert one prospect into a customer (that's your conversion rate).

• How many sales conversations do you have weekly? Monthly?
• How many sales conversations do you need to have each month in order to reach the sales levels you desire?
• Do you know what your conversion rate into actual sales is?

Customers aren't going to fall from the sky

Diana Lidstone

In a service-based business such as, health and fitness, bookkeeping or a coaching business, it's important to keep track of your daily and weekly sales conversations. I actually have a tracking sheet on my desk where I record how many sales conversations I have for the week. The more you pay attention to those conversations, they easier it the process will become.

A few years ago, when I realized I wasn't getting the sales I needed for my business, I also noticed that I wasn't picking up the phone! I wasn't having sales conversations. The truth is that you can't just do some marketing on Facebook, sit behind your desk and expect the phone to ring. Don't go to a networking event and expect that the phone will immediately ring with customers. You have to be nurture those relationships and you have to ASK for the business!

I remember listening to a business coach give a webinar several years ago and she explained that business was a little like dating. I still think it's a good analogy! You meet a prospect and you begin the relationship by asking about basic information – family, occupation, recreation, what they do for a job. You start dating. Then you might have a more serious conversation about what their challenges are. Perhaps you meet for coffee or lunch. All this is about getting to know them before you ask them to marry you (or buy from you)!

Date your prospects before you think of asking them to marry you!

Diana Lidstone

The next important gauge to monitor is your sales conversion ratio (or percentage). Imagine you are having four-to-six sales conversations a week. That's pretty good for most service businesses. How many of those conversations are converting into actual sales? 10%? 20%? 50%?

Don't panic if you are new to sales conversations and your conversion rate is low! Most people start out with a conversion rate of between 1:3 and 1:5. But with some mentoring and practice, everyone improves that number over time. The important thing is not to take it too seriously or be too hard on yourself. Just think of it as practice!

Knowing your sales conversion ratio is important to help you plan out "how" you are going to meet your sales goals. You need to know how many customers it will take to reach those 90-day or annual targets! How many new clients do you want in the next 90 days? Based on your current sales conversion rate, calculate how many sales conversations you need in the next 90 days in order to get the number of new clients you need during that period.

ROADBLOCK #6: Shifting Actions

Using the list below as a starting point, determine which gauges you should be monitoring:

GAUGES	FREQUENCY	MY NUMBER
Sales	Daily, Weekly, Monthly	
Expenses	Weekly, Monthly	
Profit	Monthly, 90-days	
Cash Flow	Monthly	
Sales Conversations	Daily	
Sales Conversion Rate	Monthly	
Email List	Monthly	
Social Reach	90-days, annually	
Inventory Levels	Monthly	
Other		

Section 3
Your Driver's Seat

ROADBLOCK #7: The Wrong Driver

In 1995, I started a bricks and mortar gift store with basically no money and very few business skills. I knew that 95% of businesses fail during their first five years. I knew it would be a struggle. It wasn't easy! I worked weekends and evenings and I spent very little time with friends or family. Vacations were rare. But after a few years of working extremely hard, over long hours, things started to turn around and the business started to make money. Woohoo, I wasn't one of those statistics!

During the time I owned my retail store, my husband held a demanding corporate job, and both my children were in their teens. That was a challenge in itself! Oh, and I should add that menopause and all its glory were ratcheting up the stress level. Just as my business hit the five-year mark, my daughter became seriously ill and was bedridden for seven long years. It was horrible. Everyone in our family was affected. Then I hopped on to the emotional rollercoasters that delivered me through my father's illness and death, and the unexpected death of my brother. It was a tough seven years!

ROADBLOCK #7: Every business owner has two inner voices; the inner critic and the inner wise person. To be successful, the entrepreneur must be aware of which voice is driving the business decisions and must ensure that the inner critic is kept to a minimum.

Everyone has a struggle story

I share these tidbits with you not for your pity or sympathy, but so that you understand that every business owner has her struggles. But from struggles come growth. I learned much of what I'm going to share with you here is what I learned during my daughter's journey to wellness.

Imagine, if you will, that your vibrant, energetic 14-year-old daughter gets up one morning feeling unwell. You think nothing of it. She's a little dizzy and she's tired. So you think, "Of course she's tired! She's a straight A student, she's on the basketball team and the soccer team, she's in Girl Guides and she's a role model to others. A day off won't hurt her."

But this one day of illness, turns into weeks, months and, eventually, years. My daughter was diagnosed with Chronic Fatigue Syndrome (CFS) and she was bedridden for seven years. It seemed like an eternity of doctor's visits, trips to the health food store, and researching her disease online. Thank goodness for the internet.

During her worst times, this previously active child couldn't walk up the stairs, hold her head up during dinner or even get out of bed. She was so tired she couldn't concentrate long enough to read a paragraph. There were no teenage dances for my daughter, no boyfriends and, in fact, no school. It was a horrific time. It seemed as though her teenage years were gone, as was the future I had imagined for her.

Eventually, I found other local mothers with children in similar situations and we formed a support group. One of the mothers, who actually had two children suffering from CFS, heard of a cure in England. She took her daughter there for treatment and, upon returning, the girl went back to school! Within the space of five months, all of us took our children to England and today our children are, well — living "normal" lives.

This bedridden child of mine was lactose intolerant, on an organic diet and taking hoards of supplements. She left the Montreal airport for England in a wheelchair and came home two weeks later almost running through the airport pulling her own luggage! How was this possible?

How was it possible that, upon her return to Canada, she booked a ski trip and went skiing at Whistler! How was it possible that, with no special pills, operation or medical intervention, she left for university and ultimately completed a Master's degree? How was it possible that, after her Master's degree, she took a six-month travel sabbatical? And today: she is living the life she loves with a full-time job she loves!

A Miracle

How was this transformation possible? It wasn't a magic pill or even a medical treatment. My daughter's astounding recovery had its roots in a scientifically proven training program based on the mind-body connection. Her transformation was founded in the concepts of neuroscience and neuroplasticity which are becoming much more main stream today. (The actual name of the program is The Lightning Process - lightningprocess.com)

Both neuroscience and neuroplasticity are fancy words for sciences related to the functioning of the brain. Specifically, it was originally thought that our brain was static – in other words it didn't change. However, today, scientists know that our brain is designed to change throughout our lifetime. In his book, *The Power of Neuroplasticity*, Shad Helmstetter explains that the initial discoveries in this area were made by helping stroke victims regain the use of muscles they once thought useless by literally teaching them how to rewire and retrain their brain function. Today, in many fields of personal growth and business, you might hear people talk about limiting beliefs, and mindset and about the mind-body connection.

So let's step back to my daughter's situation. In her case, the trainer made us aware that these participants originally had a significant amount of negative self-talk about their illness and their life situation. (I'll never get well again; I'll never do 'this' again; etc.) In other words, it had become almost habit for participants to have a tremendous amount of negative self-talk. The trainer showed them how to change this negative self-talk or how to repattern their thinking in a more positive way. Based in a combination of neurolinguistic programming, self-hypnosis and behavior modification, this training had a HUGE impact even after one day and we saw a significant change in our daughter. We called it a miracle.

I will admit that my daughter's example is certainly extreme. And she has since worked consistently to adjust her negative inner voices. But I've learned that we all suffer from "negative" thinking to some degree. We all have a negative choir that sings to us, more loudly at some times than at other time times. I've watched my daughter, I've studied rewiring, and I've started studying mindset. I've realized that limiting beliefs are the ONE thing that holds most of us back from realizing our true potential.

So let's reflect for a moment. If this negative thought process was strong enough to affect my daughter this way, is it possible that, unbeknownst to you, it is showing up in your life and affecting your business? If my daughter could go from creating sickness to creating health, do you think that changes in your mindset—your thoughts—could help you create a more profitable business? I know it could. Since my daughter's recovery, I've begun to notice how strongly our mindset affects everything in our lives and our businesses.

My inner critic

I started my coaching career just as I was approaching 60. I was re-inventing myself. I had built several profitable businesses before, but I still had huge doubts. What was the problem? The things I told myself. The problem was that the inner critic sang so loudly that I wasn't believing in myself. I became paralyzed by self-doubt.

It seems that part of the problem was that previously I had sold "stuff" in my shop. Selling "things" is much easier than selling your own services. It became apparent that my own self-doubt was holding me back. I was letting my inner critic drive the car! I didn't really need another training course, or a different business coach. There were tons of people out there who were willing to pay for my services, if only I believed in myself! That inner self-critic stopped me from creating a strong clear message at networking events, from having sales conversations and from being confident enough to close sales conversations.

I won't say that I don't have any negative chatter today, but I do work on reducing the volume continuously! I also see my old self in many, many others who struggle to build profitable businesses. They are allowing that inner critic (or as I like to call it – the "Itty Bitty Shitty Committee") to drive their businesses. That committee is sitting in the driver's seat, instead of their own brilliant self.

It is possible to get back into the driver's seat.

Four Steps to Get YOU Back in the Driver's Seat

STEP 1 - VISUALISE very clearly what you want from life.

You've heard how Olympic athletes visualizing accepting the gold medal on the podium. You've heard of mountain climbers visualize reaching the peak. They don't focus on how they are going to get there, they focus on the end result. They visualize their success as having already happened!

I used the same method when I wanted to increase my one-on-one coaching clients. I practised visualizing that I was printing off paid invoices from new clients. I focused on the joy I was feeling, and the sense of accomplishment.

What do you want to accomplish? *You sold a $1 million dollar property, you are speaking on stage in front of thousands of people.*

What's your dream?

_____

How can you visualize it with feeling?

_____

Name the feeling (emotion) you want to have. Then imagine it.

_____

_____

STEP 2 - BECOME AWARE.

The second thing that successful people do is to become aware of their negative thinking. You might hear some people say that they don't have negative thoughts! Most often, those are the people for whom the negativity has become the new normal and they don't even realize it. The first step to becoming aware of your inner critic is to listen to the spoken words you say. Not only is it true that "what you think about you bring about" but, also "what you talk about you bring about."

Sometimes I have to laugh out loud because I can hear the words my mother said time and time again: when I was a child, and I didn't think I could accomplish something, she would constantly tell me: there's no such word as "can't." Becoming aware of the words you say out loud is the beginning of becoming aware of your inner critic...the words you say out loud are representative of what you are thinking. Other words that imply negative thinking are: should, must, never, wish, want, try, just, problems. Start listening, really listening. Check what you are saying and catch yourself.

STEP 3 - REPLACE the negative words with positive ones.

It is very common today in life and business coaching to talk about negative thoughts or limiting beliefs. These are beliefs that we tell ourselves over and over again. They are assumptions, not reality, but they feel like they are real. They are typically based on our past experiences, perhaps based on something we were told many years ago by a parent, teacher or friend.

So let's examine some of the negative thoughts and feelings that we might have and see how we might replace them with more positive words and sayings:

Original Statement:	Replace with:
I'm not good enough	I love and approve of myself
I can't charge that amount	My clients easily pay me for my services
I'm afraid	I can do this - watch me!
I can't make phone calls	My clients love hearing from me by phone
I don't have any self-confidence	I decided to be me and approve of myself as I am
Others are more talented than I am	I am good enough!
I just need another training	I have all the knowledge I need within me!

Many of you have probably heard of positive affirmations. Whether it's listening to tapes, CDs or writing out your own affirmations, it all certainly helps. But just saying affirmations isn't the whole answer. (Download *Powerful Affirmations for Women Entrepreneurs Who Are COMMITTED to Grow, Prosper & Succeed* at www.dianalidstone.com/bookresources.)

STEP 4 - REPEAT WITH FEELING/EMOTION

There are two keys to making affirmations effective enough to replace your limiting beliefs:

Number One is REPETITION. You want to think about your affirmations several times a day (consistent repetition). The more the better. Personally, I find that taking 5-10 minutes at the beginning of the day, and a few minutes at the end of the day, can be instrumental in making these changes.

Number Two is to FEEL them. Just as we did in the earlier visualization exercise, it's important to add emotion to your affirmations. It's not enough just to say these affirmations! You have to create that sense of joy, gratitude or exhilaration.

An example of this four-step process might look like this:

Close your eyes and imagine your clients paying you handsomely. You are printing an invoice for a very large amount – see the amount – feel how proud you are of this accomplishment. Where is this in your office? Put yourself into the space, the light, the sounds, your feelings. Say to yourself – "I am successful. I am successful." Add more and more emotion each time. You are almost swelling up inside. Notice that you are actually smiling. Feel how marvelous you feel.

It takes practice and commitment to do this work. Louise Hay, author of *You Can Heal Your Life*, recommends mirror work (saying your affirmations in the mirror to yourself). She also notes that you might have to say your affirmations several hundred times a day. Perhaps this sounds like a lot of work, but imagine taking control of your business because you—and not your Itty Bitty Shitty Committee—are back in the driver's seat.

As you go through your day, whenever you have a negative thought, I encourage you to replace it with a simple, powerful phrase such as:

- I am the power in my world
- I can do whatever I set my mind to doing
- I am successful
- There are plenty of clients who are willing to pay me

Now you can see that there might be an inner critic driving your business, causing you to be stuck, and repeating patterns that don't serve you well. I've given you some ideas about how you can rewire/repattern those thoughts. I wanted to share another tool with you because it deals with the person who is your "other half." As much as the Itty Bitty Shitty Committee speaks to you, you have an Inner Wise Woman who most of us don't tend to listen to as often as we should.

Introducing a Second Driver

In *The Greatness Guide*, Robin Sharma says that "we were all born great." Somehow you might have forgotten about that side of you. I call your inner greatness your *Inner Wise Woman*. You know her well, although you might not hear her. She is you, your future self. The older, wiser, more calm you. She is the more courageous you, 20 years from now. She is simply your best parts, played bigger.

This technique is adapted from Tara Mohr, author of *Playing Big*, and I've used it with great success with clients who get stuck because their inner critic is constantly yelling at them. I've included the guided visualization here. Feel free to modify it to fit your circumstances. I also recommend that you record this in your own voice and then listen to it.

1. Find a quiet spot.
2. Turn off your phone or other distractions.
3. Find a pen and paper or journal.
4. Give yourself permission to spend 20-30 minutes to listen to the recording and another 20 or so minutes to journal afterwards.

Imagine you are taking a road trip in your car. It's a warm sunny summer afternoon. The sun is on your face and the wind is blowing in your hair.

You are about to travel to the future in your car. Five years ahead: whoosh! Then 10 years: whoosh! Now 15 years ahead: whoosh! And finally now you are 20 years from today! It is _____, 20__.

You drive your car down a street – it's 20 years in the future and you are about to drive up to a house where you will meet your Inner Wise Woman.

You look around and you start to notice your surroundings ... look around:

What does the street look like? What is the neighbourhood like?

You turn into a driveway ... in what kind of house does your Inner Wise Woman live in (two storey, bungalow, bungalow, side split, mansion)? What type of landscaping is around the house?

You make your way to the door and you are a little nervous.

As you approach the door, you see that your future self is coming to the door to warmly greet you and welcome you. What does she look like in terms of her hair, clothes, and demeanour?

She invites you inside. Notice what the inside of her house is like. Is it warm and cosy? Messy but homey? Do you notice any smells or fragrances?

Notice as she offers you something to drink and something to eat.

She brings you to one of her favourite spots in the house for a chat. She is present and ready to listen to you and share with you. Ask her what has mattered most to her over the past 20 years. She may answer you in words or just with a feeling or a facial expression or images. Listen to what she has to say.

Ask her: What do I need to know in order to get from where I am to where you are? Listen to her answer.

Ask her: What will help me to sing my true song? Listen to her answer.

Now go ahead, you can ask her other questions, big or small.

Now, bring your visit with her to a close, knowing that you can come back and visit her anytime. Thank her for the wisdom and guidance she's offered you.

It's time to make your way outside and once again you get into your car to drive home. Turn around and you will see that she is getting smaller and smaller. You have left that time frame and are coming back to the present.

15 years: whoosh!

10 years: whoosh!

5 years: whoosh!

And you are back to now (insert current date)

Slowly come back into your body – feel your toes – your fingers. Breathe In and out. And, when you're ready, open your eyes.

Take your journal and write down your impressions, thoughts, discoveries.

I encourage you to revisit your Inner Wise Woman regularly as she is the best of you. Let her take the driver's seat more often! Ask her to gently move the inner critic aside. The more often you trust her, the stronger your belief in her/you!

Sometimes we can have everything right: our message, our market, our marketing method, and so on, but still there is something holding us back in our business. Just ask yourself – is it possible? Is it possible that you could use some help to overcome those negative beliefs? Would you benefit from some support to listen more often to your Inner Wise Woman? Is it possible that there's some inner work to do to get you from where you are now to where you want to go?

ROADBLOCK #7: Shifting Actions

1. Complete this sentence:

   I am going to become more like my Inner Wise Woman by becoming more _____.

2. I am going to become more aware of my negative thoughts and words. The words I use most that don't serve me well are: _____

   _____

3. I commit to spend _____ minutes a day improving my thoughts and my world.

4. My new Inner Wise Woman mantra is _____

   _____

   _____.

   (For example: I am successful. I am the power in my world.)

5. PRACTICE: I will regularly journal about what I want from life, and where I want to go. And I will never forget to be thankful for the things I have.

ROADBLOCK #8: The Money Monster

You don't have a business without paying clients. That also means that you don't have a business without money. Business is about money coming in and going out. And yet money seems to be a very difficult subject for many small business owners to talk about, especially women. When I'm working with clients, often the first roadblock that we have to root out is the money monster!

ROADBLOCK #8: Limiting beliefs around money are often a HUGE roadblock for small business owners and that's why it's called a Money Monster. You have to tame your monster to be successful.

Personally, I have my own money issues and most of them are related to my feelings of poor self-worth (now that's not easy to write in a book!) So, over the years, I've tried to over-compensate by spending: spending to look better, spending to make my house look better, spending to learn more so that I'll seem smarter ... I've learned these things about myself. But that's not all.

More honesty: I tend to do a lousy job of keeping track of my money. It's not that I don't know how! For Pete's sake, I passed a university-level accounting course! I used to handle the family finances. I know how to do it. So, luckily for me, I have a very understanding husband who helps me stay on track and monitor my business dollars. Are you someone who avoids tracking your business money? Do you procrastinate about it? Or perhaps you have someone to take care of your tracking—a bookkeeper, etc.—but you don't regularly pay attention to your profits or cash flow?

Something else I've learned about myself is that I have trouble asking for money. When I started selling from the stage (as I do for my own live events), my speaking coach pointed out to me that my voice shakes, my posture changes and that the power and energy I had 10 minutes previously dwindles to nothing. When I lose confidence in myself, needless to say, so do others. It's almost like my daughter at her first attempt to drink hot chocolate after years of being perceptively lactose-intolerant! But she overcame that, and I've overcome my difficulty asking for money! You can too!

I've also learned that I undervalued my services for years. I remember the first workshop I offered: I charged $25 per person. My first coaching client paid me peanuts. However, each time I raised my rates and someone bought from me, I gained confidence in my self-worth. You can, too!

I'm sharing all of this in the hope that you recognize a little piece of yourself in my story. I want to change the way women, women entrepreneurs, and other small business owners feel about money—how they charge for their services and, lastly, how they pay attention to their money. Without these transformations, women won't be able to grow profitable businesses or live the life they truly desire for themselves or their families!

If you aren't paying attention to the dollars coming in and out, if you haven't raised your prices recently, if you have trouble asking for money during a sales conversation, and if you aren't confident with your own business money, then I strongly suggest you need to master your money monster! Welcome to the club.

I could write endlessly about this roadblock. But that's not the purpose of this chapter. The purpose is to get you started on a path to tame the money monster that is sabotaging your business and to help you make a decision around forging a new path. So we are only going to touch the tip of the iceberg here—there's so much more.

What is Money?

Many of us have grown up feeling that money is a taboo subject. Even though we don't realize it, money brings up emotion—either pleasure or pain!!

So what is money? Money is simply a tool. A tool for making choices. Money is simply something we receive or give in exchange for a service. Becoming rich, wealthy, or successful, isn't about the money. It's about what money can give us. We want money so that we have choices: choices around where to send our kids to school; choices about what type of lifestyle we live; choices over the type of vacation or car we enjoy. And yet, almost daily I meet business owners who aren't paying attention to their money gauge. These are smart people who don't know how much money they make in a month, or if their business is even profitable...until, that is, they take their shoebox of receipts to their accountant at the end of the year! I can't tell you how often I've seen really, really, smart people—people who are incredibly good at their craft, whether they work as a financial advisor, a massage therapist, a real estate agent, a coach, etc.—but they can't seem to build a profitable business.

As Oprah says, what I know for sure is that you have to have a love relationship with money to grow a profitable business. Most of us don't! Many of us avoid it; some of us like to spend it; others just don't think they need it. These are our money beliefs and these limiting money beliefs keep us broke and playing small. They keep us under-earning!

Today, I continue to work on my money problems. I've worked with mindset coaches, I've read a library of books, I've gone to conferences, and I've paid attention to my business money. Although I'm not finished my own work, I think it's important to share this with you so that you can start your own journey. Otherwise, you'll never have a profitable business. You'll become one of the 95% who fail in the first five years. Guaranteed! You see, the power to change your financial situation is YOUR power. You have the power to control your life and your business.

Money and You as a Child

Our money problems all started when we were children. Our money blueprint is simply a culmination of our whole life of experiences. That's right! Our money voice was actually formed by events, and experiences from our past, especially in our childhood. Children are extremely impressionable between zero and seven years of age. They believe that the things their parents say or do are true, and they believe that the collective beliefs of other friends and family members are also true. We grew up believing that those experiences in our life were true for everyone.

As a child, you didn't have the ability to say "yes" or "no" to a money situation; you didn't have the opportunity to determine if you agreed with it, or whether it was right or wrong. You simply absorbed the money situation (what you saw, heard, experienced) and developed a definition for yourself that defined money as...this thing. Perhaps, money was talked about in your family; perhaps there was a devastating money event when you were young; perhaps your parents didn't spend money on you, only on someone else. There are lots of reasons for your money blueprint and in this chapter, we are going to uncover them so that you can Shift into Rich.

The beliefs that you have around money are causing issues in your business, just like they did in my business. They are showing up in things like:

- Poor cash flow
- Things you do with money (or don't do)
- A dislike of talking about money (or sales)
- Fear around anything related to money
- Difficulty answering sales objections (that was my favourite)
- Continual underearning
- A tendency to be busy but not profitable

What I've learned along my money journey is that there are root causes to your beliefs around money and when you shift your relationship with money so that it flows to you easily, when you learn how to master your beliefs around money—instead of allowing money to master you—then you'll have a huge shift in your business!

Mastering Your Money Monster

Remember, I said earlier that growing a profitable business is part inner work and part outer work. There are two steps I want to share with you in this chapter. First: you need to recognize that you have a money problem—yup. There are exercises that will help you see what you might have been missing.

Secondly, I encourage you to make a decision that "Enough is Enough!" You're going to make a change. You are tired of being broke, of not having enough, and of not reaching your financial goals! I want to encourage you to draw a line in the sand. From this day forward, you are committing to shifting into rich!

I also realize that as we go through these exercises, it may be really uncomfortable for some of you and I totally understand. However, if you allow yourself to work through these money discussions, it will become easier. (Always remember, if you are feeling discomfort that means that you are probably growing, and that's a good thing!) The following exercises may be the most important thing you do for your business growth!

Exercise:

STEP 1 – What do your money issues look like in your business?

Here are some questions to ask yourself around money.

Do you recognize yourself?

A. What have you been avoiding in your business around money?

• How many invoices have you not sent out or processed?

• How many discounts have you given lately?

• Have you raised your prices in the last 12 months?

• Are you avoiding having sales conversations?

• Do you feel uncomfortable having sales conversations?

• Do you frequently negotiate downwards or give away products/ services?

• Are you avoiding asking people to join your programs?

• Are you avoiding asking for money?

• Are you avoiding recording your sales and expenses on a weekly basis?

B. What do you wish you were doing more of in your business with respect to money?

• Having more sales conversations?

• Working less hours for more money?

• Putting more dollars into your retirement fund?

• Paying down your debt?

• Earning really big money?

C. Finish these sentences with the first words that pop into your head. Don't look for the "right" answer—there aren't any. (Adapted from *Overcoming Underearning*)

My biggest fear about money is _____.

My father felt money was _____.

My mother felt money was _____.

In my family, money caused _____.

Money equals _____.

I'm afraid if I had more money, I would _____.

In order to have more money I need to _____.

If I could afford it, I would _____.

People with money are _____.

The way you were raised, including things you saw, heard, and experienced, directly affect how you are operating with money as a business owner. Should I repeat that? The way you were raised, including the things you saw, heard, and experienced about money directly affect how you are operating with money as a business owner!

The important thing to recognize here is that the way you treat money now, in your business and perhaps your life, is NOT your fault. It's no one's fault. It just happened. However, you can do something about it. You can take back your power. Let's dive a little deeper into your family money blueprint.

STEP 2. What was your family experience around money in your past?

A. What did the people in your family say about money when you were growing up? Perhaps you heard phrases like:

❑ You have to work hard to make a lot of money

❑ Money doesn't grow on trees

❑ Rich people get their money the wrong way (through stealing, etc.)

❑ Only shop the sales rack

❑ Eat your dinner – there are people starving

❑ We don't have the money for THAT

❑ There was NO talk about money, only hushed whispers behind your back

❑ Other: _____

B. What was money like for you and your family as a child?

❑ I never thought about money, it was always there

❑ My parents fought about money

❑ Father started several businesses but never succeeded

❑ Mother divorced and money was scarce

❑ Can you remember specific situations/circumstances

❑ Other: _____

C. How did your parents spend the money they did bring in?

❑ My father was tired from working and my mother spent it

❑ There were no family vacations

❑ I never saw money; I have no idea

❑ They spent it on themselves – or gave it away – or saved it

❑ I never lacked for anything

❑ Other: _____

D. What you heard, saw and experienced about money as a child has a strong impact on your current relationship to money and how money shows up in your business in some way. If you can start to work through what this is for you – it will help you understand WHY:

- Why you are doing certain things in your business
- Why you might be avoiding paying bills
- Why you might be avoiding raising your prices
- Why it's scary to have a sales conversation
- Why you haven't created a program – because that means you will have to sell it
- Why you have difficulty at networking events
- Why you hate other forms of marketing

STEP 3. What is your current money voice?

A. The past events you've experienced have created your inner Money Voice. I bet that, if you listen closely right now, you can hear that Itty Bitty Shitty Committee say something like:

- I'm not good enough to charge that amount.
- I don't need money
- I don't do it for the money
- If I don't pay attention to it, I don't have to deal with it or talk about it
- Having money isn't something to be proud of
- Money is dirty
- If I spend money, I can buy recognition/attention.
- If I don't spend money, I will seem responsible

B. What is your own CURRENT money voice?

_____

_____

_____

_____

STEP 4. How is your current money voice affecting your biz now?

None of these inner Money Voices serve your business well. For most coaches, consultants, professionals and other experts the number one ROADBLOCK holding them back from business growth and success is their Money Monster. Until you deal with the root cause of your money issues, and then change your inner money voice, you'll stay where you are! It won't matter that you've invested years in perfecting your marketing message, or thousands of dollars on your website, or years developing a client list – you won't get to Successville with the Itty Bitty Shitty Committee in the driver's seat. It's time to listen to your Inner Wise Woman who says – You are Enough!

_____

_____

_____

STEP 5. What is your new Money Mantra?

Earlier you learned that your brain can be rewired. We can change our thoughts and our limiting beliefs. With respect to money, you can create a new MONEY MANTRA. What is a new MONEY MANTRA? It's a positive affirmation that's created for your personal situation! Something that you can easily remember. It's something that you can repeat over and over again. It is something you can easily read before sales conversations. It will help you "act as if" the money mantra were true.

_____

_____

_____

One suggestion is to write it out (or print it) on several large pieces of paper and place it around where you can see it – office, bathroom, etc. Whenever you hear that inner MONEY VOICE, repeat your new MONEY MANTRA! Over and over again! Just like my daughter had to rewire her brain from sick to healthy. It was a HUGE REALIZATION for me when I discovered that I'd only be able to change my business once I changed my beliefs!!!

Okay – let's start digging into your inner money voice. The best way to explain this is by an example:

EXAMPLE:#1— Client #1

1. What is your biggest money issue now in your biz?	I worked too many hours for the pay I was receiving.
2. What is the past money experience of your family?	My father worked really hard and never seemed to get ahead
3. What is your current money voice	You have to work really, really hard to be successful
4. How does this affect your biz?	I worked all the time – didn't learn about delegating or leveraging Even though my business was successful,- I didn't have a life!
5. Create your new money mantra.	Success comes easily to me and I live the life I love!

EXAMPLE: #2—Client #2

1. What is your biggest money issue now in your biz?	Not enough clients
2. What is the past money experience of your family?	No money conversations; it's something that is only discussed behind closed doors
3. What is your current money voice	Money shouldn't be talked about
4. How does this affect your biz?	I always felt like I was apologizing when asking for higher rates or when having a money conversation
5. Create your new money mantra.	I am proud to talk about money and my value!

Now it's your turn...

1. What is your biggest money issue now in your biz?	
2. What is the past money experience of your family?	
3. What is your current money voice	
4. How does this affect your biz?	
5. Create your new money mantra.	

I know it's difficult to work on this sort of problem by yourself. After all, I didn't figure my _hit out by myself, so I shouldn't expect you to! Please remember, I'm always here to support you.

Making the Decision

So now you know the truth – the money issues that are showing up in your business aren't your fault AND you have the power to change them!

*"You don't have a problem to solve,
you have a decision to make"*

Robert Schuller

You've now come to a fork in the road. Are you going to continue on the path of under-earning, of being paid less than you deserve and of avoiding money issues OR are you going to commit to taking the other path—the one where money is your friend, where money comes easily to you, and where you've decided to play bigger and earn more?

Which road will you take? When I made the decision—the commitment—to turn my business into a profitable six-figure coaching business, I stated my decision. I wrote it on a piece of paper and looked at it every single day. Every action I took during the day was aligned with that decision. Then, and only then, did it become more than a wish; more than a dream.

What's your decision?

• Eliminate debt – how much debt, by when?
• Fund your RRSP - how much, by when?
• Purchase a new luxury car - by when?
• Earn $5,000/month; $10,000 per month; $50,000/month – by when?
• _____ by when _____

Now is the time for you to make more money!

This year I will make $_____

How does writing this out make you feel? A little nervous? Scared? Satisfied? I wrote those words out and placed them in my office. Every day, I look at them. They are my guiding light. I will and I can. And I'm always asking, "What do I need to do today to make those words come true?"

If you've gotten this far in this book, and done the work, woohoo! Congratulations! Happy Dance! It tells me that you are committed to your business. It tells me that you are in the 1% Club! You are part of the 1% that will do whatever it takes to get to Successville.

START WITH YOURSELF

When I was young and free and my imagination had no limits, I dreamed of changing the world.

As I grew older and wiser, I discovered the world would not change, so I shortened my sights somewhat and decided to change only my country.

But it, too, seemed immovable.

As I grew into my twilight years, in one last desperate attempt, I settled for changing only my family, those closest to me but, alas, they would have none of it.

And now as I lie on my deathbed, I suddenly realize: If I had only changed myself first, then by example I would have changed my family.

From their inspiration and encouragement, I would then have been able to better my country and, who knows, I may have even changed the world.

Author Unknown

ROAD BLOCK #8: Shifting Actions

1. Work through your own money story and create your NEW MONEY MANTRA.

2. Make the decision that you will no longer tolerate underearning! Write it out.

3. Identify 3 things that you will do differently with your business money starting today:

   i) _____

   ii) _____

   iii) _____

Six Rules for Achieving Amazing Results* (adapted from Overcoming Underearning)

1. Make a vow to yourself: UNDEREARNING IS NO LONGER AN OPTION.

2. Keep your commitments. If your money commitment is to pay off your debt—do it!

3. Enroll your spouse, significant other or business partner in this process.

4. Put yourself first. Remember, flight attendants tell us that in an emergency we must put the oxygen mask on ourselves first!

5. Rigorously observe your actions and thoughts!

6. Do what you dread.

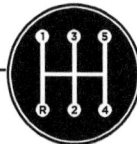

ROADBLOCK #9: Playing Small

ROADBLOCK #9: Many business owners play small; they don't see their own brilliance and they hide their genius. You were put here on earth to share your genius. Believe Bigger.

When I first met Nancy, she was struggling to earn a consistent profit in her business. She was a certified professional organizer and a member of her industry's professional organization. She attended regular networking events, and she had a very small number of clients that were paying her a small fee by the hour. She was well-schooled in marketing. Yet her business still wasn't showing a profit. Nancy was frustrated.

Fast forward to today and Nancy is a sought-after expert in her field. She transformed her business by sharing her own powerful story. Nancy's business changed and gathered momentum when she stopped playing small and started recognizing her unique strengths and skills.

You see, Nancy had been blessed with ADHD, as were other members of her family. Initially, however, she didn't see this as a blessing; she was actually ashamed of it. And yet, over the years Nancy had developed unique coping skills to handle her ADHD and that of her family. She had researched special tools to help ADHDers stay focused. She had implemented systems to make homework time easier. She knew how to help ADHDer's stay on track and on time – no easy feat!

The more Nancy and I discussed her uniqueness, the more she realized that she had not only a unique skill but also a compelling story to share. It was a slow process because Nancy didn't believe in her greatness. She tentatively spoke about ADHD. And each time she got a positive reaction, her confidence grew. Soon, instead of "selling" organizing packages like so many other professional space organizers, Nancy started to speak about helping students, families and entrepreneurs with ADHD. She was finally able to stand up as a voice for others with this often crippling condition. She gave talks to groups. She spoke at networking events. She stood on stage. She felt fulfilled that she was able to help so many people. Her business grew and prospered! Nancy soon went from broke to booming!

Stepping Up

Perhaps you don't have a story as compelling as Nancy's, but I know that you have greatness within! Nancy is an example of how to use your uniqueness to solve problems for others. Her uniqueness let her stand out in a crowded market place. No longer was she just another "professional organizer" (or financial advisor, or real estate agent). Nancy was able to answer the biggest question in her prospects' minds: "Why should I choose you?" People immediately connected with Nancy because her story was authentic and she told it with compassion. Prospects immediately knew that she could help them. Creating clients for Nancy was suddenly so much easier.

So why are we reluctant to play from our uniqueness? To some extent, we are conditioned from an early age to focus on our weaknesses. At school, we are graded by report cards and told to improve those areas where we are weak. Study harder and get better marks in math or science! So we struggle to improve in the areas where we are lacking. But when was the last time that a student was told to continue to work on their English writing skills because they were good at it?

The same happens in the workplace. In larger corporations, employee performance is generally reviewed each year. Your boss might point out areas where you need to "improve." He might have said something like, "You didn't play well with others so you should improve your leadership skills." Or perhaps you didn't _____. There's always something you aren't good at that needs improvement.

Stop playing from your weaknesses. Discover your greatness and work to improve it, strengthen it, and then play from it! The world needs your brilliance. You were born to shine!

The truth is that we do our BEST work when we play from our strengths, our brilliance! We do our best work when there's an intersection between a problem that someone has that they are willing to pay for AND our strengths.

So why would you want to play from your strengths? When we play from our strengths, we find it "easy" to do [that thing that we do]. Many years ago, I remember meeting a lady in a networking group who thought that social media was so easy! She even said, "It's so easy, why would someone pay me for that?" Well, she ended up creating a very profitable social media business! When it's easy, you feel more fulfilled and you do your very best work. Imagine, doing work that was easy!

When we don't play from our strengths, we are playing small, accepting insignificance. That's common for women. We don't want to stand out. We feel that it's the same as boasting or bragging. We often let others take our power away from us. And yet, men are able to stand in their power. As women business owners, we must identify our strengths, learn to incorporate them into our businesses and feel proud about it!

What Are You Good At Doing?

We all recognize that everyone is inherently good at something. Some things come easily to us. However it wasn't until a few years ago that I heard of various "strengths" tests that were easily available on line for a nominal fee. Now I recommend to all of my clients two tests: Strengthsfinder (Buckingham/Clifton) or Sally Hogshead's Fascination Personality Test. I highly encourage you to take both of these tests:

1. *Now, Discover Your Strengths*, Marcus Buckingham and Donald Clifton. When you purchase the book, you get complimentary access to Strengthfinder.com profile to learn your top five strengths.

2. *How the World Sees You* by Sally Hogshead. This author presents a different perspective: from the outside looking at you. Her book is well titled. Again, when you purchase the book, there's an access code to take the profile test.

Remember, you are the driver of your business! Whether you realize it or not, your business (your brand) is a reflection of who you are. Work from your strengths, your greatness, and your uniqueness, and creating clients will be so much easier. Like Nancy, your business will transform!

Ah-ha Exercise:

Several years ago, I participated in an exercise at a networking event that was a true eye-opener for me and I continue to share it. Work through the exercise, step by step.

A. Write down the name of a person you admire _____
(They can be living, dead, family member, friend, etc.)

B. Now write down five qualities you admire in this person:

1. _____

2. _____

3. _____

4. _____

5. _____

Please complete the exercise before reading further.

C. Once you have completed this, look very carefully at those 5 qualities. Do you think you have those qualities? Of course you do. "We can only see in others the qualities we have within ourselves." What we see is a reflection of ourselves!

One of the best books I've read about Playing BIG is Tara Mohr's *Playing Big: Find Your Voice; Your Mission and Your Message.* In her introduction, Tara points out that every single one of us looks at someone with admiration.

We see someone who helps to improve local schools, someone who leads a movement or maybe writes a book that could change thousands of lives. "You are that fabulous, we-wish-she-was-speaking-up-more woman," she notes. "Playing Big is about bridging the gap between what we see in you and what you know about yourself."

It's Time

It's time to stop playing small. It's time to play from your strengths and your brilliance. I know how powerful you can be when you listen to your Inner Wise Woman, when you make a committed decision and when you get into consistent action. I know it because I wore your shoes! I was petrified of failure, of not being good enough, and of being judged. "The first muscle you have to build in order to play big is getting over people's opinion of you," says Lisa Nichols in *Abundance Now*! Accordingly, the second muscle you have to build is thinking bigger about your future (remember your *Detailed Dream*, Chapter 1).

You are uniquely brilliant in your own way!
Believe Bigger!

I mentioned earlier that growing a profitable business requires a combination of both inner and outer work. The inner work is about what you need to become in order to lead a business. The outer work is about what you need to do in order to lead a business. As women, we need to become stronger believers in our own power. We need to learn how to communicate our power.

Although the inner and the outer work are two very different things, small business owners have only recently begun to learn about this "inner work." You don't reach Successville without both the inner and the outer work!

ROADBLOCK #9: Shifting Actions

1. Take a Strengthfinder or How the World Sees You test!

2. Compare notes and discuss the results with a friend or mentor.

3. Ask yourself what other unique skills have you have acquired along the way that will help you help others?

4. Do friends, clients or others tell you that you "make something look so simple"? What is that 'something"? _____
   _____

5. Ask five friends or clients if they wouldn't mind taking a very short survey. Think of 5-10 words that people use to describe you. Put these in a list and ask your Fab Five to pick one that best describes you! You might be surprised.

6. Refer to the exercise in this chapter: what words did you use to describe the person you admired? Remember that those words represent qualities that people see in you!

7. Create a list of 5 people that you would like to hang out with on a regular basis. Include only those that uplevel you; make you feel wonderful; inspire you to reach for bigger and better things.

8. Work with a mentor/coach to bring out your BIGGER BELIEF in yourself.

It's never too late to be what you might have been!

George Eliot

What Next?

Congratulations and thank you for spending this time with me! It's been quite the journey. Your business journey may have a few road blocks, detours and even some potholes. But I want to encourage you to make a commitment to continue the momentum that you have started here. Continue this never-ending journey of improvement and progress.

Sure, there will be others who will tell you that the journey is too difficult. They will be your naysayers but they are there for a purpose: to show you that growing a profitable business isn't a smooth road. If it were, then everyone would do it. So keep going. Be more like author Debbie MacComber, who spent five years typing away on her first novel every moment while her children were at school. The family scrimped and saved, living on only one salary. However, she had a dream to sell her novels. She has now written over 150 books with several best sellers and four made-for-television films to her credit. She refused to give up, even when things were difficult. I believe you can do it, too!

Like Saving Pennies

Success is about continually moving forward, one step at a time. It's about imagining how much you might accomplish if you were to commit to taking one small step each and every day towards accomplishing your goals. If you think about it, it's a little like saving money. For 30 days, if you saved one penny on day one, and then doubled it each and every day, by the end of the 30 days, you would have saved over a million dollars. It's known as the power of compound interest. It's the same in your business. One step a day will give you the momentum your business requires.

It's my intention that the Actions to Take found at the end of each chapter will have given you the steps you need to move you forward. If you haven't finished the exercises or implemented the Shifting Actions, I encourage you to commit to going back: schedule time, and implement the steps.

Time to make a change

If you find that you are uncertain about which step you need to take, or you'd like to take a deeper dive into any of these roadblocks, or if you'd like some support as you move forward, I invite you to choose from one, or more, of the following:

- Join my mailing list so that each week you inspired and motivated to Grow, Prosper and Succeed (www.dianalidstone.com)
- Attend one of my upcoming live events (www.dianalidstone.com) and this will help give you some clarity about your next step.
- Join the Achiever's Club (www.dianalidstone.com/achieversclub) to get the business skills, and tools you need as well as the community support and accountability.
- Reach out, schedule a Clarity Call (www.dianalidstone.com/apply) and let's discuss other ways that I can support you along your journey, whether it's a VIP day, some private coaching, or a business getaway. You can email me at Diana@dianalidstone.com.

If you've made a decision to embrace change, and to reach Successville, it would be my privilege to guide you along the way. There is no need for struggle. It's up to you to decide. If success is non-negotiable for you, I want you to feel supported and empowered. I believe that each and every one of you can and will grow a prosperous business.

Eliminate the Enemy

One of the best ways to stay committed, and to stay on the right road, is by engaging the support of others who are committed to being more! Being part of a community can keep your motivation higher. Being part of a community can ensure that you don't feel alone on this entrepreneurial journey because isolation is the enemy of success! There are others out there who are facing these roadblocks, just like you are. There are others who face the same loneliness and others who want more!

That's why I created my group program, the Achiever's Club. It's a place where small business owners who are in that "Glorified Employee" or "Manager" stage can come together to learn, to be motivated and to be encouraged! Here you can get the knowledge, skills and tools you need to create an amazing inventory of happy clients and feel part of a community. This is your invitation to join me and many others on the journey (www.dianalidstone.com/achieversclub).

A group setting might not feel right for some of you. I get it! Personally, I've always gone the route of private coaching. So if you'd rather investigate private coaching, feel free to connect at www.dianalidstone.com/apply. Most of my private coaching clients are those who are transitioning from the Manager into the CEO stage and who want to double or triple their sales in the next couple of years!

I'm very excited to also offer *Shift Into Rich Biz Getaways* where a small group of seasoned business owners get away to a luxury resort to fuel our gas tanks and re-start our engines! There's nothing like spas, beaches and warm weather settings to re-energize an entrepreneur. Get away so you can look at your business from a new perspective, be creative, and get feedback!

Whatever option you choose, I look forward to empowering and supporting you on your journey to Successville!

BIG Results Require BIG Action

Diana Lidstone

Again, congratulations on reading *Shift Into Rich*! I look forward to hearing how this has affected your business. Let's play bigger together!

I want to leave you with some additional thoughts and so on the next page you will find the G.P.S. Success Alphabet.

In gratitude, and wishing you all the best,

Diana Lidstone
diana@dianalidstone.com

G.P.S. SUCCESS ALPHABET

A   Abundance is everywhere.

B   Believe you are worth it; believe you can do it.

C   Commit to turning your dream into reality.

D   Done is better than none.

E   Expect success.

F   Focus on helping others; the money will follow.

G   Gratitude (for all that you have been given.)

H   Help (give yourself permission to ask for help.)

I   Imagine your success.

J   Journal about your *Detailed Dream.*

K   Keep Learning.

L   Listen more than you talk.

M   Make marketing a priority.

N   No (the word we have to get used to hearing.)

O   OMG – I want to work with you! (something we want to hear.)

P   Patience (Rome wasn't built in a day and your business won't be either.)

Q   Quiet (take time to be quiet each day.)

R   Read daily (start with Jack Canfield's Success Principles.)

S   Sales and Self-Care are your two most important business activities.

T   Time (we all have the same amount; how you use it it's your choice how you use it.)

U   Under Earner (are you one of those?)

V   Voice (to which voice are you listening?)

W   Walk Your Talk (be authentic and honest with yourself.)

X   EXcitement (passion keeps you going.)

Y   Yearly Plan (you gotta plan!)

Z   Zig when everyone else zags!

References

Abundance Now, Lisa Nichols and Janet Switzer, Harper Collins Publishers, 2016.

Be a dog with a bone: Always go for your dreams, Peggy McColl, Hay House, 2009.

How the world sees you, Sally Hogshead, Harper Collins, 2014.

Now, Discover Your Strengths, Marcus Buckingham & Donald O. Clifton, Ph.D., The Free Press, 2001.

Overcoming Under Earning, Barbara Stanny, Harper, 2005.

Playing Big, Tara Mohr, Gotham Books, 2014.

Profit First, Mike Michalowicz, Obsidian Press, 2014.

Quiet Strategy, Tara Gentile, 2015.

The Greatness Guide, Robin Sharma, Harper Collins Publishers Ltd., 2006.

The Power of Neuroplasticity, Shad Helmstetter, PH.D., Park Avenue Press, 2013.

The Success Principles, Jack Canfield with Janet Switzer, William Morrow, 2015.

The Woman's Book of Joy, Eileen Campbell, Conari Press, 2016.

You Can Heal Your Life, Louise L. Hay, Hay House Inc., 2004.

Wealth through Workshops, Callan Rush, self published e-book.

About the Author

Diana Lidstone is a distinguished speaker and growth strategist whose flawless insights have guided a generation of entrepreneurs to the success they desire and deserve. Working primarily with coaches, consultants and service-based professionals, Diana helps her clients gain the clarity and confidence they need to build their businesses so they can put more money in their pockets and make an impact on a waiting world.

As a veteran entrepreneur who has grown five booming businesses over more than 30 years of intense dedication, Diana knows what it takes to grow a profitable small business from the ground up. Like many entrepreneurs, when Diana started her first business, she had no business experience. In 1995, she began her first retail endeavor. She had to learn about purchasing a building, hiring staff, learned about inventory turns, and ultimately grew her business to multiple six-figures. More recently, she applied her hard-won entrepreneurial skills to her coaching business and in short order moved revenues from a few hundred dollars a month to several thousand! Her no-nonsense grasp of business fundamentals transcends all industries and her understanding of the entrepreneurial journey supports all clients.

Diana's philosophy is about keeping things simple. As the Entrepreneur's G.P.S., she helps clients map out their route to success with business simple tools, so they can grow their business without working harder and longer! With this proven roadmap, her clients double their sales, substantially increase their fees, and clarify their positioning in the marketplace.

Diana works with all levels of business owners from newbies in startup to CEOs and Legacy entrepreneurs. Her strength lies in seeing the big picture of a business and helping the owner see how they CAN believe bigger, in themselves and their team. Her popular Achiever's Club, private coaching, and business getaways help entrepreneurs take their businesses to the next level faster than they ever believed possible. Entrepreneurs travel hundreds of miles to attend the large events Diana hosts so that they can learn, network and have fun.

Diana lives in Brockville, Ontario, with her husband where they spend time boating through the famous Thousand Islands regularly. Her daughter is a passionate environmentalist who lives and works in the Ottawa area. Her son divides his time between the warm weather of Central America and life in Canada as a fishing guide.

If you'd like to step off your hamster wheel or learn additional business skills to Shift into Rich, connect with Diana at Diana@dianalidstone.com.

www.ingramcontent.com/pod-product-compliance
Lightning Source LLC
Chambersburg PA
CBHW060046210326
41520CB00009B/1289